presents

250 Indie Games
You Must Play

 presents

250 Indie Games
You Must Play

Mike Rose

CRC Press
Taylor & Francis Group
Boca Raton London New York

CRC Press is an imprint of the
Taylor & Francis Group, an **informa** business

AN A K PETERS BOOK

A K Peters/CRC Press
Taylor & Francis Group
6000 Broken Sound Parkway NW, Suite 300
Boca Raton, FL 33487-2742

Printed in the United States of America on acid-free paper
10 9 8 7 6 5 4 3 2 1

International Standard Book Number-13: 978-1-4398-7574-2 (pbk.)

Library of Congress Cataloging-in-Publication Data

Rose, Mike.
 250 indie games you must play / Mike Rose.
   p. cm.
 ISBN 978-1-4398-7574-2 (pbk.)
 1. Computer games. I. Title.

GV1469.15.R67 2011
794.8--dc22   2011009333

Visit the Taylor & Francis Web site at
http://www.taylorandfrancis.com

and the A K Peters Web site at
http://www.akpeters.com

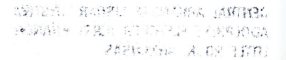

Table of Contents

Introduction

Welcome to *250 Indie Games You Must Play*—your guide to the ever-expanding and always exciting world of indie gaming. Whether you're in the know about the indie game scene or you've never played an indie game in your life, this book will help further your understanding of why indie games are so important to so many people in the entertainment industry.

Whether your usual gaming exploits involve a round of Wii Sports tennis with your family, or "fragging" terrorists in *Call of Duty: Black Ops*, the games highlighted in this book may well feel like a breath of fresh air, with concepts and ideas that will change your perspective of what video games can be.

Aside from being great fun, indie games can also be experimental, emotional, nostalgic, and occasionally just plain bizarre. Some will make you sit back in awe, while others will have you thinking "Why have I never played a game like this before?"

The games in this book represent a side of gaming that you should dabble in, and every single one is an essential experience. Better still, you can play the majority of these games for free, and even the commercial releases are incredibly cheap.

Just be warned—once you start playing indie games, you may not be able to look at your big-budget blockbusters the same way ever again.

Mike Rose
IndieGames.com Editor

What Are "Indie" Games?

The exact definition of an indie game is sketchy at best, and both indie developers and gamers argue periodically over what they believe the word "indie" signifies.

While independent games are those that have been created without the backing of a publisher, the term "indie" has evolved further and now generally refers to an independent game that has been developed with a certain "indie spirit" by a small team or an individual.

Without the pressure from a publishing deal, indie developers are able to create the exact experience they desire, leading to a massively varied selection of games. Ranging from experimental platformers that you'd never see from a big-budget developer, to the oft-discussed "art games," indie games provide unique and sometimes unusual diversions.

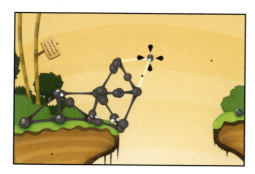

Indie developers come from all sorts of backgrounds and every corner of the globe. Some are enthusiastic hobbyists who relax after a hard day at work with a spot of game development, while others create indie games for a living. Numerous online indie gaming communities provide these developers with a place to talk shop, share their latest projects, and take part in competitions and game jams.

What Does It Mean to Be an Indie Developer?

Being indie has a variety of benefits and advantages to different developers. Here, a number of well-known developers explain what being indie means to them.

"Being indie for me means I'm not a faceless cog in a giant production line that operates for the profit of somebody else. I get to work on what I want, when I want, how I want."
>—Bennett Foddy (*Evacuation, Qwop*)

"Making games and publishing them as a young indie designer meant that thousands of people knew my name and my work before I even began applying to universities to earn a degree."
>—Greg "Banov" Lobanov (*Assassin Blue, Dubloon*)

"If you believe in a concept, you don't have to pitch to publishers or shareholders; you just plonk your arse in a chair and start building it. A 'real' definition of indie might describe work practice or organizational structure, but the spirit of indie is making stuff because you want to."
>—Jarrad "Farbs" Woods (*Rom Check Fail, Playpen*)

"I think it's telling that, instead of referring to just one particular financial model for game development, the term 'indie' is more used to denote things that are weird, inventive, or personal—games that probably wouldn't be developed by bigger or more commercial groups."
>—Stephen "The Catamites" Murphy (*Space Funeral, Paul Moose In Space World*)

"Indie games allow me to channel all my ideas and creativity, but still make enough money to get by and do some of the travelling and self-educating that I would have otherwise put off."

          —Chevy Ray Johnston (*Beacon, Skullpogo*)

"You can change the direction or scope of a project at any point or drop it altogether. There's a community of other indies out there ready to help you with any aspect of the project."

          —Mark Essen (*Punishment, Flywrench*)

"Indie game development really does cut the corporate puppet strings and lets you roam the wild west of game development. It also means rolling out of bed and hitting your head on your desk, but man, doesn't it feel good!"

       —John Cooney (*Achievement Unlocked, Maverick*)

"I've worked on a publisher-funded project before, and the publisher had the final say on whether the game saw the light of day. That was not a good feeling."

          —Jason Rohrer (*Passage, Sleep is Death*)

"People squabble over definitions like 'indie' and 'independent;' they're the new fanboys. There's now even indie sub-classes, because indie has become too mainstream. Some of these games are so indie, they don't even exist."

      —Dan Marshall (*Privates, Time Gentlemen, Please!*)

"The best thing about being independent is being able to do something I love."

         —Charlie Knight (*Irukandji, Space Phallus*)

Why Have Indie Games Become so Popular in Recent Years?

The end of the first decade of the twenty-first century saw a boom both in the number of developers getting into indie game development and the amount of attention the scene was receiving. We asked some notable developers what they thought was the cause of all this interest.

"The quality of games being produced has really shot up. Small teams are making the sort of clever, exciting things you just couldn't get from big publishers, coupled with various factors like ease of accessibility and more coverage."

—Dan Marshall (*Privates, Time Gentlemen, Please!*)

"The larger companies started to focus on big budget games, but the demand for smaller titles didn't decrease. A hole was left in the market for indie developers."

—Nicklas "Nifflas" Nygren (*Knytt Stories, Within A Deep Forest*)

"Indie games bring fresh ideas back to a video game scene that has become entirely focused on sales."

—Locomalito (*L'abbaye Des Morts, Hydorah*)

"The web created an amazing DIY publishing mentality, where anyone with a keyboard can be a columnist or an author, anyone with a mobile phone can be a film director, and anyone with a free hour or two can make and publish a video game."

—Jarrad "Farbs" Woods (*Rom Check Fail, Playpen*)

"The number of tools and available platforms has grown; additionally, the tools have gotten better and easier to use, allowing more people to make games. I think there's a growing demand among players for simple but good games focusing on gameplay."

—Jesse Venbrux (*Karoshi, They Need To Be Fed*)

"Kids who grew up with video games have now hit the 25–30 year mark, and have the opportunity to make those dream games they always talked about on the school yard a reality."

—Edmund Mcmillen (*Super Meat Boy, Time Fcuk*)

"Indie games embody the same restless drive for strangeness and excitement and constant mutation that also creates the best pop music, the best pulp fiction, the best b-movies and the best comic books."

—Stephen "The Catamites" Murphy (*Space Funeral, Paul Moose In Space World*)

"It is maybe because indie games are so personal to the author. Playing a game made by one or two people is much more intimate and human than playing a game made by a hundred people."

—Matt Thorson (*Give Up Robot, An Untitled Story*)

"Indie games feel weird, have some taste from back in the days when everybody was indie, and are made by small-time guys somewhere. All the ingredients to be trendy!"

—Daniel Benmergui (*Today I Die, I Wish I Were The Moon*)

"Like punk, indie and electronic music are tearing down the walls that separate producers and consumers. They are contributing to the de-geekification of the gaming phenomenon, reaching people and groups who wouldn't otherwise play games."

—Molleindustria (*Every Day the Same Dream, Run Jesus Run*)

"We are out there in the Wild West leading the charge. Who doesn't love a cowboy?"

—Greg Wohlwend (*Solipskier*)

Indie Gaming Resources

If you're looking to get more acquainted with the thriving indie gaming scene, look no further than the following places. These news sites and festivals play a huge part in helping bring unique, delightful, and entertaining games to the masses.

WEBSITES

 **IndieGames**. Started by veteran indie gamer Tim W., IndieGames.com is now the most popular indie gaming news site; it covers all the latest news, reviews, and releases and is updated daily. The IndieGames podcast features a prominent indie developer each week.

TIGSource. The largest online community for indie developers, TIGSource holds themed competitions that are always very popular, and the forums are the perfect place for anyone interested in creating their own games.

 Bytejacker. Bytejacker is an online review show that focuses mainly on indie games, with plenty of humour thrown in for good measure. A daily news blog also accompanies the videos.

Indie Game Festivals

The Independent Games Festival. The IGF was established in 1998 by UBM TechWeb, who also owns IndieGames.com, and is held annually at the Game Developers Conference in San Francisco. The festival highlights the best indie releases of the past year, along with the most promising projects still in development. Many IGF award winners go on to have great commercial success.

IndieCade. Celebrating indie developers from around the world, the IndieCade festival has been promoting the most diverse, artistic, and culturally significant indie games since 2005. The organisers aim to provide a gaming equivalent to the Sundance film festival, rewarding tremendous passion and innovation.

Indie Games Arcade. The Indie Games Arcade is an annual UK-based event that is part of the Eurogamer Expo. Organised by The Mudlark Production Company, the arcade highlights all the best upcoming and recently released indie games, with a particular focus on the British indie gaming scene. Mudlark also runs the indie videogame development conference World of Love.

What You'll Need to Play

So you've decided to take a dive into the world of indie games—but what will you need to play? Fortunately, there is very little effort needed on your part, although it's worth taking note of the following:

- The majority of the games featured in this book do not require a computer with more than average specifications, although there are some exceptions. For the commercial games in particular, it's worth checking out system requirements from the game's official site before purchasing.
- Every game in this book is available to download for PC, so almost everyone will have a computer at home that is capable of running these games. Certain games are also available on other platforms, such as the Xbox 360 or Nintendo Wii, and this will be stated where appropriate.
- Many of the games, especially those that are browser-based, require that you install a plug-in to your computer. Two such plug-ins include the Adobe Flash Player and the Unity Web Player. Some of the download games will also need the Microsoft XNA library installed on your machine. Any game that has these requirements will automatically ask you to install the appropriate plug-in as necessary.
- Some games are compatible with a gamepad or controller, and using this method of control can greatly increase the enjoyment you get from a gaming experience. It's recommended, but not necessary, that you purchase an Xbox 360 controller for use with your computer.
- Keep an open mind when you begin playing these games—many will be unlike any gaming experience you've had before, and some attempt to portray ideas and emotions that you may never have seen in gaming before.

Feeling prepared? Okay, let's do this—here come 250 of the most worthwhile indie gaming experiences. Note that there are thousands of enjoyable indie games out there for you to discover, and this selection is meant more as a starting point for anyone looking to explore the scene, rather than an exhaustive list of the very best indie games available.

There are three sections to pick your way through—download games, browser-based games, and commercial games. You can choose a game at random to download, or start from the beginning and work your way through the lot. There is no special order to follow, so feel free to try the games out in whatever order best suits you!

Acknowledgments

A huge thank you to all the developers whose work is featured in the book—and of course, that thank you is extended to every indie developer who helps to make the indie gaming scene as fantastic as it is.

Many thanks to my fiancée Jo and my parents for the much-needed support, and to the proofreading god that is Simon Archer.

My gratitude must also go out to Simon Carless who has been hugely supportive every step of the way, and of course to fellow IndieGames.com editor Tim W.—without him, there would be no perfect place for following the indie gaming scene.

Special thanks to Anthony Carboni who allowed me to borrow his indiegam.es url, and who is also one seriously cool dude.

Part 1

Download Games

The games in this section need to be downloaded to your computer for you to play them, and they may need installing as well. Every featured game will work on a Windows PC, but you'll need to check a game's official site for requirements if you're playing on a Mac or using the Linux operating system.

Some games may not have an official site, and will instead be available to download from a forum or a file-sharing site. This is usually the case for games that have been developed for competitions or game jams.

Star Guard

Loren "Sparky" Schmidt

Inspired by a series of stories about Mars written by Edgar Rice Burroughs, *Star Guard* follows a mysterious green spaceman as he attempts to defeat an evil wizard. Armed with just a laser gun, our hero must battle through the wizard's minions on Venus, overcoming levels full of nasty aliens and obstacles.

The game has a very minimalist feel with simple visuals and sound effects, yet play is incredibly engaging thanks to tight controls and hectic action. Every now and again our hero stumbles upon allies who are fighting for the same cause, and you can choose to keep them safe or rush past and leave them to their fates. The dialogue is kept to a minimum, with the occasional short story printed on the backdrop.

Star Guard was nominated for the Excellence in Design award at the 2010 Independent Games Festival.

http://indiegam.es/playstarguard

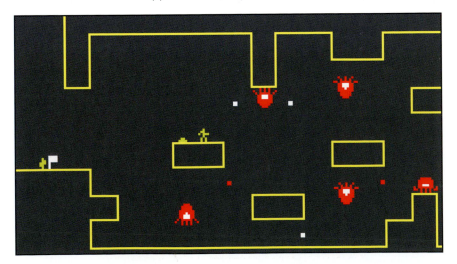

RunMan: Race Around the World

Tom Sennett and Matt Thorson

In the words of developer Tom Sennett, *RunMan: Race Around the World* is "a game about doing your best and running really, really fast." Our hero RunMan shows up for a race, only to find that the other contestants have dropped out because they fear his speed. Rather than accept the trophy, RunMan decides to challenge himself to a race around the world.

RunMan has two main actions—run, and run really fast. As he pounds along platforms knocking bad guys out of the way and popping balloons, he automatically springs off any wall he runs into, allowing for a very smooth gaming experience that many players have compared to the early *Sonic the Hedgehog* games. This game has a lot of style too, from RunMan shouting "Rock on!" as he runs to the 1920s blues, country, and jazz music soundtrack.

The game was drawn entirely in Microsoft Paint over the course of four years, and features over 30 levels to rush through.

http://indiegam.es/playrunman

Enviro-Bear 2000: Operation Hibernation

Justin Smith

"Who is driving the car? A bear is driving the car! How can that be?!"

Enviro-Bear 2000: Operation Hibernation was originally developed for (and won) the Cockpit competition on the popular indie gaming site TIGSource, and was later ported to the iPhone and the Android. You play a bear driving a car who wants to fatten himself up before hibernating for the winter. The bear can only use one paw at a time, which makes driving around an absolutely hilarious nightmare. The game is purposely awkward to control, and a variety of obstacles from vicious badgers to showers of pine cones will constantly hinder your progress. There are also other bears driving their cars and looking for fish to eat.

This game was nominated for the Nuovo Award at the 2010 Independent Games Festival and is widely regarded as a must-play indie game, especially when played for a laugh with a group of friends.

http://indiegam.es/playenvirobear

The Black Heart

Andrés Borghi

A bloodstained world exists alongside the human world, although we choose not to see it. The king and creator of this dark void has been brutally murdered, and his powerful heart—the Black Heart—has been stolen by a demon known only as Final.

Six twisted characters all want to take the heart as their own, and each is determined to battle through the bloody wasteland, taking out one opponent at a time, until the heart is won. Each character's story line is told through gorgeously grim cutscenes, which include an assortment of special, super, killer, and fatal attacks with complex button pressing that will please fighting-game veterans. There are also reams of extra game modes, including practice, team fights, and hotseat multiplayer.

The Black Heart runs on the MUGEN engine, a tool that allows developers to build masterful fighting games. Andrés Borghi spent over seven years developing the game, creating the character stripes, animations, and backdrops from scratch.

http://indiegam.es/playblackheart

Atomic Blast

Qrleon

Atomic Blast is a tricky platformer with a plethora of dangers to keep your eye on. The protagonist may have a gun, but that won't help much if he can't dodge the enemy soldiers and death lasers that will cut him up with a single shot.

On each of the 12 levels, the hero can hang from ceilings, climb through shattered windows, and unlock doors—but the enemy guards are a very real problem since they can fire at any angle and can easily pick you off whether you're above or below them. You, however, can only shoot horizontally and so are at quite a disadvantage. Once you manage to beat the tough missions there's an even trickier final boss battle to contend with.

Atomic Blast started life as a tribute of sorts to Chris Roper's *Destructivator*, and after several months of chopping and changing, eventually found its way on to the Glorious Trainwrecks site.

http://indiegam.es/playatomicblast

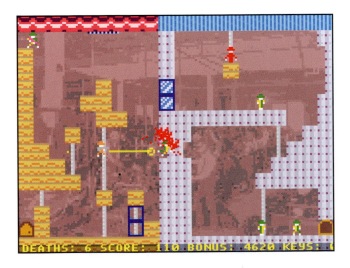

Magic Planet Snack

Kyle "Lazercatz" Tolbert

In *Magic Planet Snack*, you play as a wizard who has accidentally turned himself into a space worm. You now need to fly through space, chomping on planets and devouring other wizards for points.

There are plenty of bad guys and flashing blocks to dodge, and staying aggressive yet cautious is the best way to grab the big scores. As you eat the orbs dotted throughout each planet your HYPER meter fills up. Once the meter is full, the planet turns into cakes, pastries, and ice cream for a few seconds, during which time you'll want to grab as many as you can for a serious addition to your score.

Magic Planet Snack was originally going to be a racing game, but Tolbert says that he eventually opted for a more score-based approach so that players would "make stupid decisions."

http://indiegam.es/playMPS

GunFu Deadlands

Christiaan Janssen

In *GunFu Deadlands,* you play a gunslinger who is out to prove he has the quickest draw in the West. Enemies are scattered around on each level, and when they spot you they will immediately start firing in your direction. But you have quite an advantage over your enemies in that you can activate "bullet time," which slows the action down and allows you to focus on aiming your pistol.

Clicking the right mouse button as you run into enemy view activates bullet time, but it takes a few seconds to reload, so if there are multiple enemies you may need to take them all out during the slowdown.

A level editor is included with the game so that players can create their own shootout environments and share the results with friends.

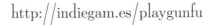

http://indiegam.es/playgunfu

Jetpack Basketball

Mark "messhof" Essen

Jetpack Basketball is a combination made in heaven: fast-paced hoop action played with jetpacks. A single player can take on an AI-controlled opponent, or two players can go head-to-head locally for some slam-dunking action.

The idea is to grab the ball, zoom up towards the basketball hoop, and let go of the ball at the correct moment, allowing it to arc into the net. When the other player has the ball, you can tap your grab button to take it away and go for the shot. You can even grab the ball just after an opponent makes a shot, and slam-dunk it to steal the point. Manoeuvring your character is intentionally difficult—just as you'd expect playing jetpack basketball in real life would be! The first player to score 11 points is the winner.

Jetpack Basketball was originally developed during Bivouac Urbain 2009, a game prototyping jam in Québec City, Canada.

http://indiegam.es/playjetpackBball

Rose and Camellia

Nigoro

A Japanese fighting game that features "the elegant art of feminine conflict," *Rose and Camellia* follows the story of Reiko, a newlywed whose rich husband dies the day after the wedding. To claim his house as her own, she must defeat the evil women who currently run the house.

One by one, Reiko must slap, evade, and counter-slap her opponents into submission. Fights are played via timed swipes of the mouse across the face of the enemy, and a scrolling rose at the top of the screen shows whether it's time to attack or to dodge. After the women of the house are defeated, it comes to light that the evil Madame Camellia has the house in her power, and Reiko must then beat her to claim her inheritance.

The action is very tongue-in-cheek with amusing animations, dialogue, and characters. A sequel—*Rose and Camellia 2*—is also available, although players must complete the original game before the sequel will unlock.

http://indiegam.es/playRandC

Clean Asia!

Jonatan "Cactus" Söderström

Clean Asia! isn't your average shoot-'em-up game. With lots of psychedelic visuals and flashing colours, the game sends two American pilots on a quest to clean up Asia after the eyes of mankind have left the bodies of their hosts and taken Thailand, New Korea, and China by force.

The two available characters play quite differently and offer distinct shooter styles. One pilot cannot shoot, and uses instead a powerful thrusting technique to break enemy ships into pieces and fire the debris into the remaining machinery. The second character plays more like a normal blaster, firing at enemies and using the broken enemy pieces to launch huge special attacks.

Clean Asia! was originally developed in two months for the Autofire 2007 competition at the SHMUP-DEV forums, and ended up winning the contest. The game is considered by many indie gamers to be one of the driving forces that shot developer "Cactus" into the limelight.

http://indiegam.es/playcleanasia

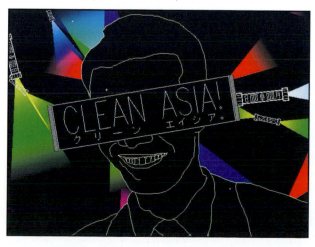

Dwarf Fortress

Bay 12 Games

In development since 2002, and still a work in progress, the first public build of *Dwarf Fortress* was released in August 2006. Since then, the game has received numerous updates and has built a huge fan base of players, all keen to delve frequently into this ASCII fantasy world.

In Dwarf Fortress mode, players manage a dwarven outpost in a randomly generated world made up of towns, caves, civilizations, and wildlife. Your army of dwarves can be sent out to find treasures scattered about the land, or commanded to craft furniture and weapons for your fortress. As the land changes over time other civilizations may want your fortress for themselves. There is a serious amount of depth to *Dwarf Fortress*, and although it can take many hours to read enough background material to fully understand how to play, it is a very worthwhile cause.

Another mode allows you to explore the land as an adventurer who recruits a band of followers and accepts quests from different towns and leaders.

http://indiegam.es/playDF

Knytt Stories

Nicklas "Nifflas" Nygren

Knytt Stories is a collection of platforming adventures that revolve around exploration and puzzles. Players can venture into the world of "The Machine," or download a multitude of excellent user-created stories for free.

The story that comes with the game follows Juni, a character originally seen in the *Knytt Stories* predecessor *Knytt*, as she attempts to save the world from a nasty machine that is sucking the life out of everything. Power-ups give Juni extra abilities so that she can move further towards her goal. Once you've completed this story there are hundreds of user-created levels available for download from KnyttLevels.com and the *Knytt Stories* forums. You can even have a crack at creating some of your own tales.

"Nifflas" himself has created additional stories, including "A Strange Dream" and "Gustav's Daughter," both of which can be downloaded from the official site.

http://indiegam.es/playKnyttStories

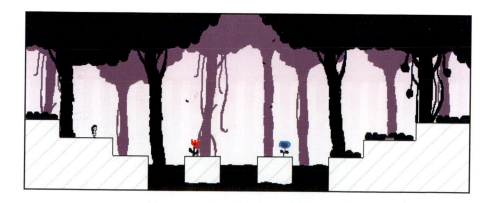

Igneous

Going Down in Flames

Developed by a student team from DigiPen, *Igneous* is a short and frantic rush through an erupting volcano in which you attempt to take control of a small tiki totem as it rolls along through collapsing stone pathways and bridges.

The incredible speeds mean that you need to think fast and keep a constant focus on the action; in each of the three levels, face-melting speeds and the threat of a dip in molten lava are always very real. Pathways disappear into the magma without warning; therefore, you'll most likely need a few play-throughs before you reach the end. Many players have commented that *Igneous* is exactly how they would like a modern, three-dimensional version of *Sonic the Hedgehog* to play.

The game is rather abrupt, clocking in at around 15 minutes of play. There is also an impossible mode with the same three levels ramped up to maximum difficulty.

http://indiegam.es/playigneous

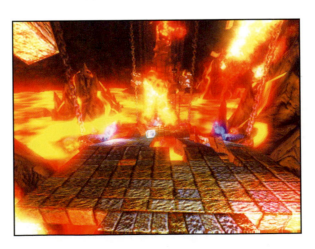

The Underside

Arthur "Mr. Podunkian" Lee

The Underside is an exploration platformer that has been in development since 2005. A preview build of the game is available for download and gives a taste of how the final release will play.

A king rules the Overside of a flat planet. When his people become corrupt and he wants to start fresh, he simply flips the planet over so that the bottom becomes the top. Unfortunately, this side also becomes corrupt and the king vows to destroy the whole world unless he can find a single innocent person. You take control of that one person, called Ip, who has been thrown into the Underside. He must journey back to the Overside and stop the destruction of the planet.

The game features humorous dialogue and plenty of silly power-ups, including life toast and invincible burgers. There's also a tool for creating your own worlds, and a couple of example mods thrown in that you can play through.

http://indiegam.es/playunderside

Lost in the Static

Sean Barrett

Lost in the Static is a platformer that may cause headaches if you stare at it for too long. Everything in the game—from the environments to the enemies to the main character—is coated in black and white static.

The game messes with your perceptions as you navigate around the various rooms; the background is constantly scrolling while the foreground either stays in one place or moves around to indicate areas or enemies that you shouldn't touch. The effect is striking; your brain perceives the background and foreground as two different planes, giving the game a three-dimensional feel. Whenever the hero dies, he explodes into static that is then swept away by the scrolling backdrop.

The game was developed over the course of four days. Developer Sean Barrett has provided modding tools on the game's official webpage for anyone who would like to create their own levels.

http://indiegam.es/playLitS

Chalk

Joakim "Konjak" Sandberg

With some clever line-drawing mechanics involved, *Chalk* is a rather unique action game with plenty of charm. The player controls a floating monochromatic hero who dodges around numerous obstacles and enemies that fly onto the screen.

Fortunately, you've got a magic stick of chalk that can be used to eradicate baddies. Enemies can be killed by drawing on them with your mouse, but each one is different and requires special disposal tactics. A helpful tutorial explains how to destroy each type of obstacle.

There are enjoyable boss battles at certain intervals during play, which usually require that you figure out how to attack first. If you earn at least an "A" rank on each of the main six levels, you'll unlock the special endurance challenge.

http://indiegam.es/playchalk

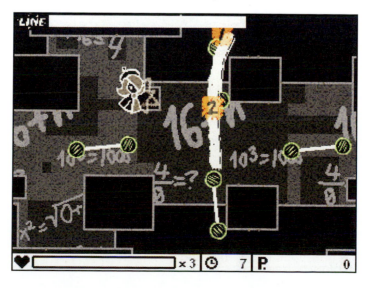

Trilby: The Art of Theft

Ben "Yahtzee" Croshaw

Trilby: The Art of Theft stars the main protagonist from Ben Croshaw's adventure game *5 Days A Stranger*. British cat burglar Trilby has moved to America in search of posh offices and mansions to plunder.

The game plays out as a series of side-scrolling stealth missions, with the goal to find the target and escape undetected. Each level features different amounts of light, and Trilby will be able to sneak around guards and crack open safes without raising the alarm if he's cautious enough. If he's spotted, a Taser in the tip of his umbrella will come in handy to prevent witnesses from divulging his location.

At the end of each heist, you're given a rank and reputation points based on how many witnesses were Tasered and how many alarms were raised. Rep points can be spent on buying upgrades to aid Trilby in future heists.

http://indiegam.es/playTrilby

N

Metanet Software

Everyone wants to be a ninja, and the 2005 indie classic *N* gives you the opportunity to fulfil this dream, putting you in control of a stick-figure man in black. He has amazing speed and dexterity, but his lifespan is also rather short, clocking in at just 90 seconds.

Fortunately, collecting gold allows the ninja to live longer, and there is plenty of gold scattered around, along with nasty hazards and robots ready to impede his progress. Players must jump, dodge, run, and wall-jump to a door switch, then escape through the exit. *N* is a game that's easy to get into but difficult to master, with character physics that take some getting used to.

The game has more than 500 levels and comes with a level editor called the NEd. *N* was granted the Audience Award at the Independent Games Festival in 2005, and as a result of its popularity a sequel called *N+* was released on the Xbox 360 Live Arcade.

http://indiegam.es/playN

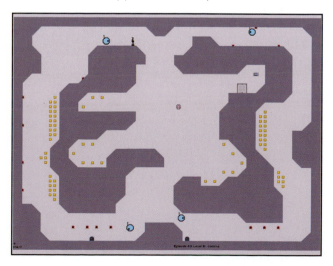

Karoshi

Jesse Venbrux

The Japanese term "karoshi" refers to situations where people literally work themselves to death—hence, Jesse Venbrux's tough puzzle platformer challenges you to kill the protagonist in a variety of ways on each level, from landing on sharp spikes to getting crushed by falling crates.

What appears to be a relatively simple game quickly shows its true colours, as the rules of play change often. While your goal is always to kill yourself, you will need to experiment with different ways of doing so by pressing buttons and shooting weapons. After completing 25 levels, there's even a boss battle that you must lose multiple times.

Karoshi proved so popular that Jesse decided to make an entire series of games dedicated to the concept, including *Karoshi Factory* (a co-op edition) and *Super Karoshi* (in which you help other characters kill themselves). The browser version of the game, *Karoshi Suicide Salaryman*, has been played over three million times.

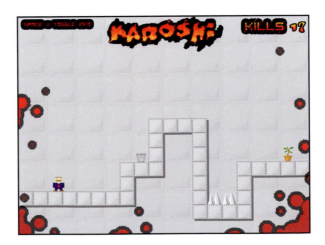

Rock Boshers

Dugan Jackson

Rock Boshers is a remake of the first-person shooter *Red Faction*. Developer Dugan Jackson has taken the story and setting from the classic game, twisted them around quite a bit, and presented *Rock Boshers* as if it were running on an old ZX Spectrum computer.

You are a British gentleman who has been tricked into travelling to Mars to do the dirty work of a large corporation. Trapped down in the mines, you seize an opportunity to escape but soon discover that the guards are the least of your worries as hordes of zombies home in on your position. There are plenty of secrets to find, including a bonus space shooter called Rockaroids. The game comes with a multiplayer arena battle mode so that up to four players can take each other on.

Rock Boshers was originally developed for the TIGSource Bootleg Demakes competition in 2008, but Dugan wasn't able to have the full game ready in time for the voting phase. Fortunately, he continued development and released the full version a couple of months later.

http://indiegam.es/playRockBoshers

Iji

Daniel Remar

Developed over the course of five years, *Iji* is well known for featuring one of the best indie gaming stories to date. Iji is visiting her father's workplace when an alien race known as the Tasen invade; Iji is badly injured and her father replaces parts of her body with cyborg parts to save her life.

Iji awakens to find all of her family dead except for her brother Dan, who gives her instructions over an intercom. Iji sets out to meet up with her brother and battles the Tasen along the way with the help of her new nano-technology abilities. She also learns of the lives of the Tasen through journals left around the facility, and must use this knowledge to choose her path.

The game is huge, with hours of gameplay, multiple storylines, and plenty of secrets to uncover. *Iji* is highly regarded and considered one of the best indie games of 2008.

http://indiegam.es/PlayIji

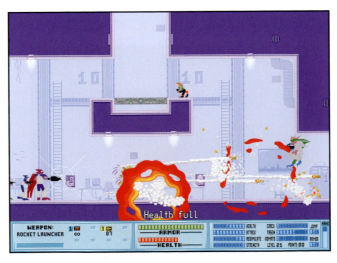

Jumper Three

Matt Thorson

Ogmo is the result of a failed experiment to create the world's most perfect life-form, and once he has been abandoned by his creators, Ogmo sets out to find his place in life. *Jumper Three* follows Ogmo as he travels into space and lands on a mysterious planet full of traps and tricky terrain that he must navigate.

The *Jumper* series is known for its intense difficulty, and *Jumper Three* is no exception. There are hazards everywhere, and Ogmo must use a combination of wall-jumping and double-jumping, coupled with quick reactions, to stay alive. Later in the game, Ogmo is able to split into different forms and to use new abilities to bypass even tougher obstacles.

Ogmo's previous journeys, chronicled in *Jumper* and *Jumper Two*, are also available for download from Matt's site. *Jumper* has proved to be a huge inspiration to indie game developers, and has influenced the development of big releases such as *Super Meat Boy*—in fact, Ogmo can be found as a hidden character in that game.

http://indiegam.es/playJumper3

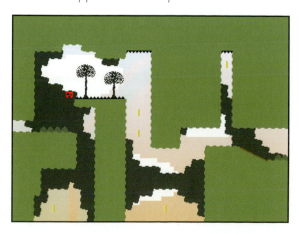

Seven Minutes

Virtanen Games

There is an odd, blue ball situated on a pedestal, and a booming voice tells you not to go anywhere near it. Of course, curiosity is a powerful thing, so you're going to jump up and grab it.

As you do so, a huge face appears and states that you have seven minutes left before the world comes to an end—all because you grabbed the ball. With seven minutes on the clock, you're left to race through an ever-changing maze full of nasty spikes and tough platforming sections. Things won't be quite as they appear, as seemingly solid walls become hollow and spikes spring out of the floor, ready to catch you by surprise.

There are two endings to the game, and the one you get depends on how you act. Finding the "good" ending may prove tricky, but the face will give you a clue about how to find it during the "bad" ending.

http://indiegam.es/play7Minutes

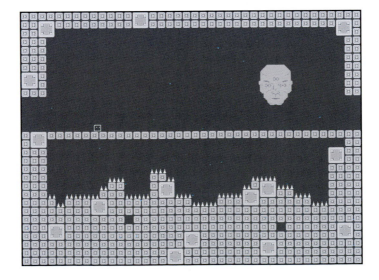

I Wanna Be The Guy

Mike "Kayin" O'Reilly

I Wanna Be The Guy: The Movie: The Game (to give the full name) is a platformer for masochists featuring The Kid, a boy who wants to be The Guy. From the get-go, IWBTG is insanely and unfairly difficult, yet it's ultimately addictive. Every single screen looks impossible at first glance, which makes winning all the more rewarding.

The game constantly attempts to trick the player, throwing seemingly simple challenges into disarray or providing areas that appear to be completely impassable. Many of the gameplay elements and environments parody old NES games such as *Ghosts 'n Goblins*. There is even a selection of characters from boss battles that have been taken straight from Nintendo games, including Bowser from *Super Mario* and Mother Brain of *Metroid*.

Numerous indie developers list *I Wanna Be The Guy* as an inspiration to their work, including Edmund McMillen and Tommy Refenes of Team Meat, the developers behind *Super Meat Boy* (The Kid was included as an unlockable character in *Super Meat Boy*).

http://indiegam.es/playIWBTG

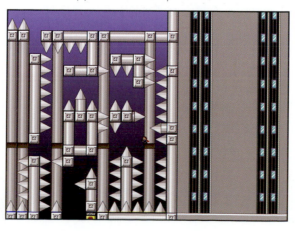

Rescue: The Beagles

Nenad Jalsovec

A cargo plane carrying beagles to an animal testing facility has crashed in the mountains, and the evil lab has sent out its researchers to collect the useable dogs and kill the rest. You take on the role of an animal rights activist who saves the beagles from harm and sets them free.

Rescue: The Beagles is a lot more complex than it sounds, as the beagles (and nasty researchers!) are on three different procedurally-generated mountains, and the protagonist needs to use ropes and parachutes to move between them. The game has a very quick-moving arcade feel as you move between levels grabbing everything available, firing owls at the bad guys, and fixing up injured dogs with medical kits.

Rescue: The Beagles was originally developed for (and won) the TIGSource Procedural Generation competition. The game features music by chiptune composer and producer Rich "Disasterpeace" Vreeland.

http://indiegam.es/playBeagles

You Found the Grappling Hook!

Mark "messhof" Essen

As far as self-explanatory titles go, *You Found the Grappling Hook!* is definitely up there with the best of them. You play a horned character who is armed with a grappling hook and must use it to swing through a series of blocky caves.

The X button controls both the hook and the protagonist's jump, so prepare to tap X a fair bit! The hook can be fired either straight up or at a 45-degree angle, allowing the hero to hang and plan the route ahead. Eventually, you'll find an axe that allows you to dig gold out of the cave walls; unfortunately, the moment you grab it the entire cave will begin to collapse, leaving you to salvage as much of the gold as you can before making your escape.

There's an online leaderboard ("The Goldenest") that lists the players who were able to grab the most gold before escaping.

http://indiegam.es/playYFTGH

ROM CHECK FAIL

Jarrad "Farbs" Woods

Developed over three weeks for the Video Game Name Generator competition at TIGSource, *ROM CHECK FAIL* splices together the retro worlds of Mario, Zelda, Pacman, and other popular game characters to create a completely insane gaming experience; one moment, Mario is jumping on the heads of Space Invaders, and the next, Pacman is running from Goombas. The backdrops display popular scenes from old console games.

Every few seconds, there is a glitchy internal computer noise, and everything in the current level stays in the same position but changes into something else. The idea is that players need to constantly change their strategies, and strategies are dependent on whatever character is currently being controlled.

Jarrad developed *ROM CHECK FAIL* while still working at mainstream game developer 2K Australia. Early in 2009, he once again used Mario—this time in a short game-cum-message for his bosses at 2K—to announce that he was quitting his job and becoming a full-time indie developer.

http://indiegam.es/playRCF

Skullpogo

Chevy Ray Johnston

Skullpogo is a game about bouncing on pigs and bats; using a pogo stick, Skullboy must launch himself up and down on the animals to build up as large a combo as possible.

As Skullboy lands on the animals, his combo meter fills, and if he lands on another animal before the meter empties, the combo increases. The idea is to get a huge combo and earn enough points to go to the next level before time runs out. Plenty of different power-ups appear in the sky for you to grab; these will speed Skullboy up and occasionally mess up the controls.

Skullpogo started life in 2002 as *Pogopher*, Chevy Ray's first-ever completed game. Six years later, the developer decided to expand on his formula and enlisted the help of friends Brittney Cloud and Marius Schneider to help him develop a more polished and entertaining product. *Skullpogo* is also available as an iPhone game.

http://indiegam.es/playSkullpogo

Space Phallus

Charlie's Games

Space Phallus is a crude yet hilarious side-scrolling shooter in which you battle against a horde of genitalia and bodily fluids. The majority of enemy ships are penises that continuously fire shots of semen in your direction.

At the beginning of each level, you'll have to hold back bursts of sperm that shoot towards you at an alarming rate. Once these are out of the way, the phalluses themselves appear, flying through the air or rolling along on the floor. There are plenty of other enemy types to be found as well, although you're better off finding out about those for yourself (especially if you're looking for a good giggle). The boss battles feature grotesque beasts that you'll want to destroy as quickly as possible.

When the going gets too tough, you'll have access to other kinds of weapons that will help to change the tide in battle. For example, your missiles can usually cut enemies down with a single shot, and the fire breath can clear whole screens full of penises.

http://indiegam.es/playSP

The Marionette

Team Effigy

The Marionette is an adventure game about a sculptor who is subjected to a strange sequence of events. Martin is partway through completing his latest work when a mysterious letter arrives in the post. Upon opening the letter, Martin loses consciousness and eventually wakes up in front of a strange house he has never seen before. With nowhere else to go, he ventures into the house to find some answers, and things get a little bit spooky.

There are a lot of twists and turns in this story, and the writing and dialogue are both top notch. The best way to experience *The Marionette* is to explore every area fully, as there may well be puzzles and items that you'll miss.

There are different endings to the story, which depend on actions chosen throughout play. Auriond, one of the developers from Team Effigy, describes *The Marionette* as "interactive fiction" in addition to its adventure game tag.

http://indiegam.es/playMarionette

Excavatorrr

Arvi "Hempuli" Teikari

Excavatorrr is a tricky digging game with Atari 2600-style visuals. You are a lonely miner who burrows deep into the ground, trying to extract as much gold as possible while avoiding death at the hands of nasty creatures in the depths.

The world of *Excavatorrr* is procedurally generated, so every time you play, you'll find that the pathways and locations of the monsters have changed. The miner can normally only dig crosswise and must find holes in the ground or use bombs and dynamite if he wants to dig downwards; ladders are available that will allow the miner to climb up again. Once you've collected enough gold, you can buy supplies in the shop on the surface. If you dig down deep enough, you'll find an assortment of surprising enemies to contend with.

Hempuli originally designed *Excavatorrr* as a Ludum Dare contest entry, but he wasn't happy with the original build. He decided to improve on the base concept and eventually released this more complete, content-heavy edition.

http://indiegam.es/playExcavatorrr

Fedora Spade

Hardi "Orchard-L" Gosal

Fedora Spade is a series of detective adventure games that play in a fashion similar to the popular Nintendo DS *Phoenix Wright: Ace Attorney* games. Fedora Spade has been assigned to lead a failing unit in the police force, but the work becomes meaningless and Spade starts to hit the bottle to drown his sorrows. A last chance to save his career comes in the form of a challenging case.

Players look through the case file and then interrogate the murder suspect, using available evidence to question inconsistencies in the suspect's statements. The game features a fantastic story with lots of clever twists and humour throughout.

A total of four *Fedora Spade* games were released over the course of two years, and each presents a new case for Fedora to investigate while revealing more of his mysterious past. All four games can now be downloaded as a package along with the *Fedora Spade* original soundtrack.

http://indiegam.es/FedoraSpade

The Legend of Princess

Joakim "Konjak" Sandberg

In case it wasn't obvious from the title, *The Legend of Princess* is a *Zelda* fangame that was created by renowned indie developer Konjak. Many argue that this side-scrolling homage plays just as well as the two-dimensional *Zelda* games of old.

Elements such as a similar soundtrack, collectable hearts and rupees, flying chickens, and exploding Bombchus have created a love letter to the Nintendo classic. Yet Konjak has added his own personal touches to the genre, in the form of fantastic action-packed swordplay, satisfying explosions, and great level design. Also, there are a number of different weapons and items that can be chosen before the game begins to alter how challenging the gameplay is.

No *Zelda* fangame would be complete without some great boss battles, and in this department *The Legend of Princess* does not disappoint. It is truly one of the best fangames ever released.

http://indiegam.es/playLOP

Jumpman

Run Hello (aka Andrew McClure)

What appears to be a rather simple platformer gradually shows its true, wacky colours in *Jumpman*. You take control of an orange stickman who must traverse multiple "paths," each with its own set of game rules. The first few levels are simple, which allows you to get used to the overall concept and slippery movement. Yet soon all hell breaks loose.

To reach the finish, you'll be playing around with strange physics-based movement, rotating levels around 360 degrees, and generally becoming utterly confused as infinite repeating patterns appear all over the screen. The next level is always shown in the background of the current maze, as if to taunt you with the difficulty you will soon face.

Developed over the course of a year, this game comes with a level editor for creating your own insane masterpieces and a "playground" that acts like a version of Microsoft Paint—but with the orange protagonist jumping all over the place.

http://indiegam.es/playJumpman

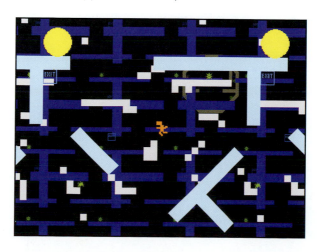

Beacon

Chevy Ray Johnston

Winner of the Ludum Dare 15 competition, *Beacon* was developed in less than two days and follows the story of a child who is lost in the darkness. A beacon of light appears out of nowhere, and the child must follow the light closely or else be sucked into the blackness.

As the beacon floats along, you'll need to jump over chasms, swim through underground pools, and dodge deadly spikes. Now and then the light will take a course that you can't follow, and you'll have to use the light from nearby crystals to work your way back to the beacon. On later levels, the beacon will begin to glide more rapidly, so you'll need quick reactions if you want to keep up.

Beacon is a great achievement in that players will likely feel genuine terror during the action, which features scary background noise and dark creatures moving around. You will really feel a bond with the beacon by the end of play.

http://indiegam.es/playBeacon

Glum Buster

Justin "CosMind" Leingang

Developed over a period of four years, *Glum Buster* is an abstract adventure game with minimal storytelling and many areas to explore. The explanation of what players are supposed to be doing is limited, and the game leaves you to experiment with the protagonist's powers.

Once sucked into his gloomy sphere, the hero can fire shots of lights via the mouse buttons. He roams the huge, surreal world opening up paths and interacting with the surrounding creatures. Puzzles are usually solved by testing out each of the different powers with world elements until positive results are found. In parts of the game, the hero is floating around, while other parts play out as platformers.

The environment's lack of definition and negligible amount of dialogue allows players to create their own stories and logic, although the introductory scene suggests that the boy has been pulled into this *Glum* world for moping about while his friends have fun in the rain.

http://indiegam.es/playGB

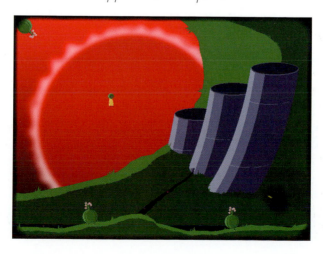

Focus

Jesse Venbrux

Focus is a platformer with a teleporting twist. The main character escapes from a cage and soon finds a glowing gem that gives him the power to move quickly through space and even pass through solid objects.

When the focus button is held down, a blue circle appears around the hero and time slows down. During this period, he can choose a destination point and then appear at that point with appropriate momentum behind him. Focus mode is great for reaching areas that are high up, since the hero can enter it multiple times before he must touch the floor. However, the blue circle shrinks the longer you stay in this mode and will only be restored when you touch the floor again.

Note that you may want to set your focus key to Ctrl rather than to the space bar, as Windows may not allow you to press the space bar and two directional keys at the same time.

http://indiegam.es/playFocus

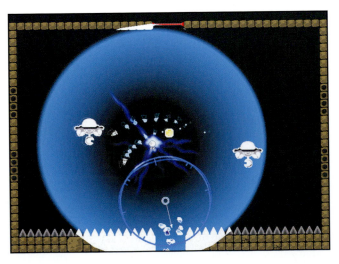

Assassin Blue

Greg "Banov" Lobanov

You are Blue, a highly skilled assassin working for an unknown organisation. Armed with your trusty blade and capable of some great swordplay, you are given targets you must locate and kill—although you're never told why these people deserve to die.

Assassin Blue can lunge and guard to beat his opponents, and can also perform a special attack on enemies who shield themselves. At each level, Blue must leap over rooftops and wall-jump up shafts to reach his goal. There are a number of different targets that can be destroyed for special bonuses, although some are hidden away and must be sought out. As the game progresses, Blue learns that he has a rival assassin called Red, and the story then starts to take an unexpected turn.

Whenever Blue reaches his specified target, a boss battle ensues; these battles require that you watch how the enemy moves and attack whenever there is an opening.

http://indiegam.es/playAB

The Manipulator

Virtanen Games

There are a group of people who call themselves Manipulators, and one of them has managed to infiltrate a mysterious weapons base. The Manipulator cannot fight, and must take over the mind of another person and use it to forge a safe path.

You control your enemies once their minds have been taken over, and you can make them shoot other enemies, making it safe for you to progress. You can then either leave the bodies unharmed and continue on your way, or be an evil soul and make the bodies explode. There are multiple endings, each of which depend on how you handle yourself during gameplay.

The game also gives you the power to read the minds of your hosts and to see details from their lives, such as whether they are married or have children—a power that might have been included to influence whether you decide to be a good or evil Manipulator.

http://indiegam.es/playManipulator

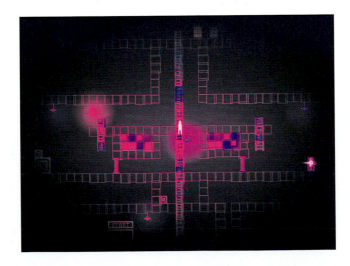

Saut

Mabi Games

If you enjoy tough platformers, *Saut* may well surprise you with its simplicity. It's a gorgeous one-button experience in which any button on your keyboard will make the little hero hop along (and most likely fall down into pits many times over).

How long you press your preferred button determines whether the little man makes a short bound or a lengthy leap. However, *Saut* is more about momentum than anything else. The protagonist slides after each jump, and the idea is to position him so that his slide takes him right up to the edge of a drop. You then use his momentum to leap across wide gaps. There are numerous opportunities for precise jumping, since *Saut* includes lots of short platforms and dangerous manoeuvres.

Saut was developed in under a week for the Gamejolt Minimal Contest. If you're able to collect every special coin in the game, your final score will be entered into a secret VIP leaderboard.

http://indiegam.es/playSaut

We Want YOU

Quicksand Games

We Want YOU puts a satirical spin on the subject of war by asking you to fight for your country and your people, while at the same time providing statistics and news flashes that demonstrate why "war is hell."

You take control of a soldier descending through time and killing enemy troops along the way. The world is procedurally-generated, so each time you play, the path is completely different. As you progress, news bulletins provide up-to-date titbits about what is going on around you and the game's textures change to fit the current climate and era. There are frequent twists and turns along the way, and the enemy gets tougher as the technologies become more modern.

Make sure you give this one a few good tries—it really gets interesting once you reach the second part. There is an extra mode to unlock if you can get far enough.

http://indiegam.es/playWWY

Being Struck by Lightning...

Mabi Games

The game's full name is *Being Struck by Lightning Is Probably the Best Way That You Could Die on Account of All of Its Awesomeness*. The game is as tricky as the title is long-winded, with tough jumps to make and numerous dangerous spike pits.

Initially, the platforming isn't too much of a problem as you leap and bound over danger and dodge the ambling bad guys. However, the action quickly gets really tough and you'll need to make precision jumps with expert timing and tight movements. On each level, your goal is to reach the storm cloud and get yourself electrocuted by the lightning bolt. The level design is really quite harsh towards the end of the game, and only the most masochistic players will survive the challenge.

Being Struck by Lightning was developed for a Gamejolt contest with the theme "Shocking," and won The Probably Best Way That You Could Die on Account of All of Its Awesomeness Award for its efforts.

http://indiegam.es/playLightning

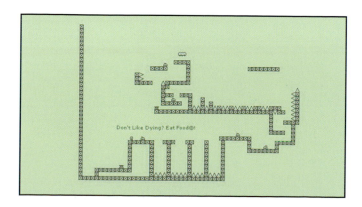

Devil's Tuning Fork

DGE Team

All around the world children are falling into comas and scientists don't know the cause. *Devil's Tuning Fork* takes place inside the mind of a coma victim who is trapped in a strange reality that must be escaped.

You are armed with a special tuning fork, and you click to sound the fork and reveal the surrounding area through visual sound waves. Along the way you must collect oversized stuffed animals that represent other children trapped in comas and sound bells to open doors and continue along the path. There are also rooms that require you to right click to emit a low frequency wave that can detect broken floorboards. There's a very dark tone to the game, with eerie and sometimes frightening noises emanating out of the darkness.

Devil's Tuning Fork was developed by a student team at DePaul University and inspired by M.C. Escher's optical illusions. The game was a finalist in the 2010 Independent Games Festival Student Showcase.

http://indiegam.es/playDTF

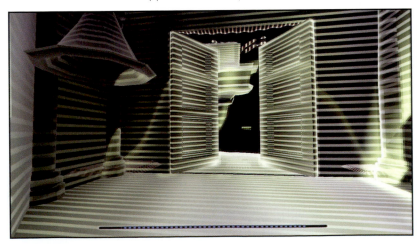

Takishawa is Dead

Andrew Brophy

A dangerous criminal called Takishawa is on the loose, and a reward has been offered for his capture. In an odd world full of characters who have televisions for heads, you set out to find Takishawa, dodging traps and navigating difficult platforming sections along the way.

Takishawa is Dead features numerous areas made up entirely of black-and-white blocky surroundings, where you talk to various individuals. Many of the areas will require you to hop across platforms and jump over spikes, but fortunately there are frequent save points so that you're never thrown back too far when you die. If you manage to reach the end of the game, there is a rather big twist to the story waiting for you.

The game was featured on many popular mainstream gaming sites at the time of release. As a result, developer Andrew Brophy began work on a sequel called *Takishawatwo* (not yet released at the time of writing).

http://indiegam.es/playTakishawa

Rara Racer

Stephen "Increpare" Lavelle

Rara Racer features a rather unique concept: someone is watching a play-through of a game called *Rara Racer* on YouTube, and you are controlling the game in the YouTube video while an announcer (voiced by developer Lavelle himself) provides audio commentary on your playing.

The game in the YouTube window is an intentionally dull top-down racing game that's about driving around cones—but it's what goes on around the video that makes *Rara Racer* so unique. Browser pop-ups block your view of the game until the "viewer" clicks to close them, and instant-messaging chat windows display short conversations in an attempt to distract you. The entire game is made to look like someone's computer screen (including a Windows toolbar at the bottom), and the game even ends with the user "shutting down" the computer.

Developed in less than 48 hours for the Ludum Dare 13 contest, *Rara Racer* took home first place and was highly praised for its innovative concept.

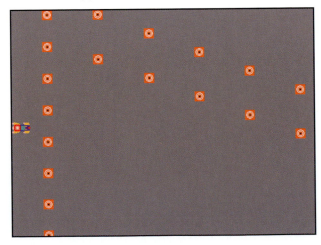

Descent

Ted Lauterbach

Descent tells the story of an unnamed hero's journey into the bowels of a dark and mysterious cave. As he drops deeper and deeper into the darkness, a disgusting brown blob follows closely behind, advising him to turn around and return to the surface.

The protagonist can fall from any height without getting hurt and can also cling to ledges to assist in climbing. The game's mystery revolves around what you'll discover at the bottom—is the strange, ugly creature telling the truth, or trying to keep you from finding something amazing in the depths of the cave? Without giving too much away, you should note that you'll need to prepare yourself once you've reached the bottom.

After you've played through the game, it's worth trying again, but this time follow the monster's advice and see what happens. By the way, the monster's taunts were inspired by the passive-aggressive nature of GLaDOS from the popular platform-puzzler *Portal*.

http://indiegam.es/playDescent

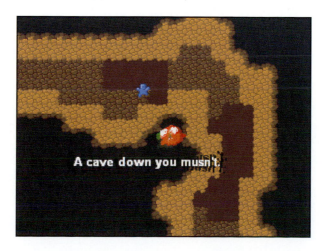

Chaser

Connor Carpenter

Developed over a couple of days, *Chaser* is not what it first appears to be. Players are presented with a simple black environment and take control of a green man chasing a turquoise figure. Over time, you'll pick up speed, grab coins that the turquoise man throws out, and eventually trip and come to a standstill.

The main question throughout play is whether or not it is possible to catch up with the fleeing guy, and by exploring this concept you may well find the ending to the game. The underlying message could be interpreted as follows: sometimes it's best to violate life's edicts instead of mindlessly following the rules.

With a unique visual style and a wonderful soundtrack that builds up as your character moves faster, *Chaser* is a quick and simple "art game" that is well worth checking out.

http://indiegam.es/playChaser

Queens

Nathan "noonat" Ostgard

Queens is a very short but difficult platformer about a ruthless king who throws his many wives into a dangerous gauntlet whenever he tires of them. You lead each queen through the obstacles in the run and try to stay alive.

Each section relies on trial and error; you'll constantly find yourself dying in unfair circumstances. However, as each new queen is thrown into the pit, you can use your prior knowledge of traps to push on and reach further areas. The king watches as you make your way through the hazardous caverns, giving the action a very eerie feel. Through perseverance and some serious skills, you'll eventually be able to lead one of the queens to victory and make sure that the king never harms anyone again.

The game was developed over the course of three days for the tenth Mini Ludum Dare competition. The theme of the contest was domestic violence.

http://indiegam.es/playQueens

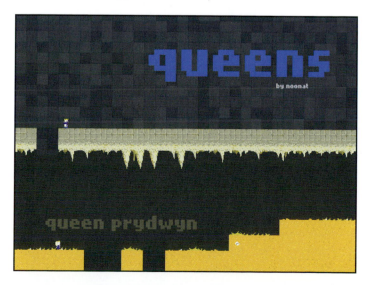

Din

Team Bill

If you've ever tried to have multiple conversations at the same time, you know that focusing on what is being said can be tricky. *Din* puts you in the shoes of Billy, a popular guy who everybody wants to talk to. Unfortunately, everyone wants to talk to him at the same time and will get upset if he doesn't respond appropriately.

As people crowd around you making small talk, occasionally one will ask you to press a key on your keyboard. Pressing the correct key in time will earn you points, while pressing the wrong one—or ignoring the person completely—will deduct from your score. The game is simple enough at the beginning, but once you've got a crowd of six different people talking over each other, it's very difficult to understand what they're saying!

Din was created for the Global Game Jam, a 48-hour development jam that takes place all over the world. The team consisted of Teddy Diefenbach, Mansa Gory, and Brian Lee.

http://indiegam.es/playDin

FallOver

Arvi "Hempuli" Teikari

FallOver puts a humorous spin on the side-scrolling Mario games. The British gentleman protagonist is on a mission to collect coins and reach the white flag, but he has quite a problem with keeping his balance. If he lands on the edge of a platform, ambles into a rock on the ground, or walks off the side of a mound, he'll topple over, cursing in all sorts of British slang.

The key to surviving is to land centrally on each platform and avoid any spinning blocks or bad guys. If you do happen to topple over, you can simply press the A key to stand up again, although you can only do this three times before you're forced to restart the level.

There are coins to collect throughout each stage, and while these are not essential, you'll earn a perfect score if every single one is grabbed before the end.

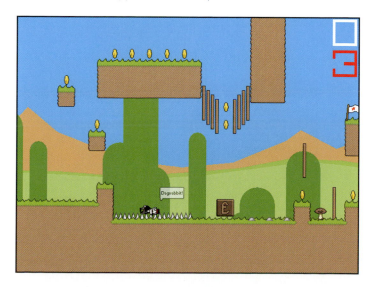

Dungeon

Jonatan "Cactus" Söderström and Arthur "Mr. Podunkian" Lee

When *Dungeon* was first released, there was a fair amount of confusion amongst indie gamers. Some reported completing the game easily with a low number of deaths, while others were experiencing a variety of problems ranging from issues with jumping to slippery character movement. Was the game broken for certain people?

It turned out that the game was indeed riddled with bugs that were deliberately added by the developers. Random impediments that depended on the Windows username of the player were layered on the gameplay, making the game difficult to play for some and completely impossible for others. The day after the game's release, an explanatory file called "Clarity" was released, which revealed the bugs and showed players the issues that would affect their playthrough.

Dungeon was developed in two days for a Mini Ludum Dare contest as "an amusing experiment," according to Jonatan. A bug-free version of the game is available for download.

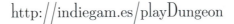

http://indiegam.es/playDungeon

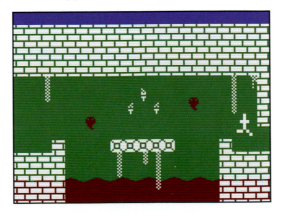

Cave Story

Daisuke "Pixel" Amaya

Cave Story—or *Doukutsu Monogatari*, to give its original Japanese title—is a huge side-scrolling platform game that was in development for more than five years. The hero wakes up in a cave with no memory of how he came to be there. Upon finding a small village, he learns that he's on a floating island populated by creatures called Mimigas and by an evil doctor who is hunting the Mimigas down.

As the protagonist begins to explore the surrounding areas, he stumbles across a whole cast of characters: from Sue Sakamoto, a girl who has been turned into a Mimiga, to Curly Brace, a female robot. The story is nice and long and features a satisfying number of experience levels and lots of new weapons for players to find. Make sure you pick up the English translation patch by Aeon Genesis, as the original download features Japanese dialogue and interfaces.

In addition to the free PC version, there are commercial updated editions for the Nintendo Wii and Nintendo DSi available for purchase. The commercial editions feature new visuals and some exclusive gameplay modes.

http://indiegam.es/playcavestory

Gravity Bone

Brendon "Blendogames" Chung

Citizen Abel: Gravity Bone (the full name) puts you in the role of a secret agent as you attempt to complete a couple of undercover missions from a first-person perspective. Nuevo Aires, *Gravity Bone*'s world, is incredibly striking and stylish, with cube-headed characters and unusual level design. The gameplay is simple yet clever.

Missions are provided by your organisation via cards, and range from dressing as a waiter to serve your target a special drink to taking photos of birds and jumping across flagpoles. While the game is rather short, progression is very enjoyable and there's a great twist at the end. At the time of release, many gamers commented that it felt as though *Gravity Bone* ended a little abruptly, and there is still hope that Brendon will release a sequel one day.

The game runs on the Quake 2 engine—although Quake 2 is not required to run it—and features music from the 1985 Terry Gilliam film *Brazil*.

http://indiegam.es/playGravityBone

Awakener

Ben Chandler

Awakener is a short but entertaining point-and-click adventure set entirely in one area. You control Fadi as he tries to help his Aunt Sylvia wake up and remove a mysterious stranger from outside her inn.

The puzzles are quite straightforward, which allows you to enjoy the humorous and bizarre dialogue. Among the strange and wonderful characters who inhabit the level you'll meet a man selling pennies for a dollar, an assassin who is waiting for a message, and a cleric who will only talk in scripture. Since the game is rather brief (clocking in at around 20 minutes of play), it's worth going through each dialogue tree and checking out each reaction, as there are plenty of laugh-out-loud moments to be found.

Now and then, Fadi references the fact that he is in a video game, and at one point he mentions *Shifter's Box*, another one of developer Ben Chandler's releases.

http://indiegam.es/playAwakener

Back Door Man

Edmundo Ruiz and Francisco Gonzalez

Back Door Man follows the exploits of a male prostitute on a not-so-typical work night. While drinking at a bar after hours, the protagonist gets talking to the bartender and begins to describe each of the night's affairs.

There are three "jobs" in total, and you can play through each in any order you fancy. Each job has a strange storyline with multiple endings that depend on how you act during gameplay. Once the escort has told all of his sordid tales, he leaves the bar and will encounter one of a variety of different final game endings—the one you receive is determined by how you completed each of the three jobs. *Back Door Man* is a short game that's worth playing through multiple times to find all the different conclusions.

The game was created for the TIGSource Adult/Education Compo, hence the adult theme. As you'd expect, the game features profanity and nudity in abundance.

http://indiegam.es/playBDM

Paul Moose in Space World

Stephen "the catamites" Murphy

Paul Moose in Space World is rather special in that every character, item, and backdrop you see in the game has been created by hand—mostly with paper and pens—then photographed.

Paul himself is drawn on a piece of paper, and glides along as you tell him where to go. *Paul Moose in Space World* is an adventure game with a very *Hitchhiker's Guide to the Galaxy* vibe throughout; it's quite short, but the witty dialogue more than makes up for the brevity. Eventually, Paul meets an alien who happens to be made of plasticine—a substance that is very alien indeed in Paul's papery world.

Paul Moose in Space World was developed for a Gamejolt Contest with the theme "Axioms" and took the second-place prize. The game used the adage "A picture is worth a thousand words," referring to Paul's comical conversations with the alien.

Dreamside Maroon

Terraced

Voyages to the moon would be so much easier if we simply followed the guidance of the scarf-wearing hero Aster from *Dreamside Maroon*—this little guy rides there on a sprawling vine.

Holding up his mysterious lantern, Aster can cause the vine on which he sits to grow outwards, twisting and winding all over the gorgeous night sky. There are other lanterns along the way that light up when Aster gets close; these attract swarms of fireflies, which can be collected for a temporary speed boost. Eventually, the fireflies light up the entire area, allowing you to progress. *Dreamside Maroon* is a beautiful sight to behold, and once you've created a huge spiral of vines, it's great to turn around and see your creation.

The story is told via snippets of poetry that set the scene perfectly. Developed by a student team from the DigiPen Institute of Technology, *Dreamside Maroon* was chosen as a finalist for the 2010 Independent Games Festival Student Showcase.

http://indiegam.es/playDreamside

Super Crate Box

Vlambeer

Super Crate Box flips your concept of scoring on its head, as collecting takes precedence over killing. Crates appear on each level, and you score points by grabbing them while dodging the bad guys who descend from the top of the arena.

With such a simple premise and setting, you'd expect *Super Crate Box* to be a walk in the park, but it's quite the opposite. Each time you grab a crate, you're granted a random weapon—however, while some of the weapons are powerful, others are incredibly weak and fiddly. Killing baddies does not earn you points, but if you allow their numbers to build up, they'll turn red and storm around the level at twice the speed. Therefore, it's worth shooting these ugly beasts along the way.

The game is very content-light, yet only the most quick-witted players will be able to unlock every mode available. *Super Crate Box* was the first release by Vlambeer, a Dutch games company set up by developers Jan Willem Nijman and Rami Ismail.

http://indiegam.es/playSCB

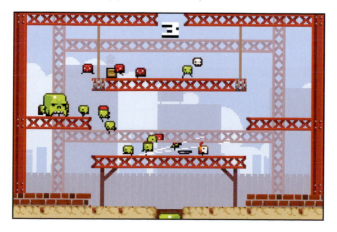

Pathways

Terry Cavanagh

Pathways explores the idea of interactive storytelling through abstract decisions and literal pathways. The hero walks through the same town each day, taking different routes and encountering separate stories that, when all brought together, make up his life story.

With each new beginning, the protagonist's wife tells him that she worries whenever he goes out on one of his walks. You're then given a choice of multiple paths to walk down, and after you've reached the end of the day, you're thrown back to the title screen where your tally is increased. Once all eight endings have been found, the game draws to a close. Whether you take each story literally or as a metaphor for one of life's many twists and turns, there's no denying that *Pathways* emanates an incredibly heartfelt atmosphere.

Pathways started life as a 48-hour Ludum Dare contest entry, but developer Terry Cavanagh decided to take the concept further and ended up spending more than two months developing the game fully.

http://indiegam.es/playPathways

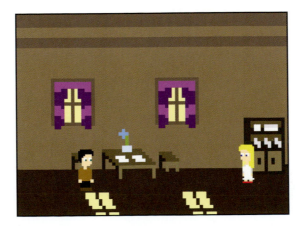

Octodad

DePaul University Student Team

Developed by a student team in Chicago, *Octodad* is one of the funniest games you'll ever play. It's an adventure game about an octopus pretending to be human, who even lives with his seemingly oblivious human wife and kids.

The control scheme is even more mental than the storyline. The octopus's two squid-like legs are controlled separately by clicking and dragging the corresponding mouse buttons. Pressing your space bar allows you to enter Arms mode and grab items (most likely causing lots of accidental destruction). Given the deliberately awkward controls, your octopus will roam around his house in a very comical manner, trying to live his life as normally as possible so that his family doesn't uncover the truth.

Due to its hilarious concept, the game was covered by the majority of mainstream gaming sites when it was released. It was also selected as a finalist in the 2011 Independent Games Festival Student Showcase.

http://indiegam.es/playOctodad

The Journey Down

Theodor Waern

The Journey Down is an episodic adventure game with a graphical style inspired by the classic LucasArts adventure games of the '90s. Bwana and his friend Kito run a gas station and find themselves in a predicament when the electricity company threatens to cut off their power supply.

Coincidentally, a young woman happens to walk into their workplace that day looking for a book and she offers Bwana and Kito good money if they can find the book for her. The game plays out exactly like classics such as the *Monkey Island* series, with left-clicks that allow Bwana to move and interact with things or people, and all inventory items stored away at the bottom of the screen.

At the time of writing, only the first episode in the series, "Over the Edge," has been released. Four chapters in total are expected, with "Episode Two: Into the Mist" coming in the summer of 2011.

http://indiegam.es/playJourneyDown

Space Funeral

Stephen "the catamites" Murphy

Space Funeral is a surreal and very silly role-playing game that follows Phillip, a man who cannot stop crying (although we never discover exactly why this is the case). Banished from his home, he eventually meets up with Leg Horse and sets out to the city of Forms.

The gameplay is distilled down to the most manic form, with short, simple dungeons to overcome and easy enemy battles that you can even skip by using an "auto" option. From your attacks to your character statistics, almost nothing is explained, but it doesn't really matter as the focus is entirely on your journey and the people you meet.

The dialogue is hilarious but somewhat terrifying, especially since the game has an unhealthy obsession with blood; the title screen presents you with BLOOD, BLOOD, and BLOOD as your three options, and you'll constantly be picking up bags of blood that have been dropped by enemies. At one point, you'll even take a raft trip down Blood River.

http://indiegam.es/playFuneral

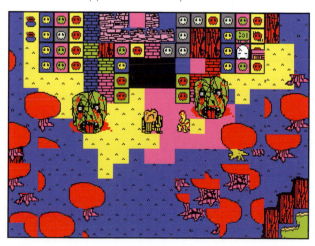

Jables's Adventure

Jason "JaJitsu" Boyer

It's not often that you wake up to find a squid on your head, especially one who pronounces you a hero. This is the story of *Jables's Adventure*, which features cephalopod Squidric leading Jables through a series of heroic deeds.

Jables's Adventure revels in observing that it's all just a game, and characters frequently make references to this fact. At the beginning, Jables can only run and jump, but eventually he finds a weapon and is able to venture farther into more dangerous regions. Along the way, there are boss battles to overcome and an abundance of fruit to eat, and the dialogue between Squidric and Jables gives the whole experience a rather charming vibe.

Developer Jason Boyer created the game, which has a full soundtrack from Kevin Carville, over the course of a year. Boyer's other well-known indie title is called *Cat Poke*.

http://indiegam.es/playJables

L'Abbaye des Morts

Locomalito

Set in the 13th century, *L'Abbaye des Morts* (translated as *The Abbey of the Dead*) follows a Cathar called Jean Raymond as he attempts to escape from the Crusaders. He finds refuge in an old abandoned church that soon is revealed to have a dark secret.

The visual style and level design take inspiration from classic Spectrum ZX games of old such as *Manic Miner* and *Jet Set Willy*. Jean must dodge enemies as he ventures into the bowels of the church catacombs to collect crosses. Since he has no way to attack, he must solve puzzles to navigate around hazards. Parchments scattered around provide clues as to how to obtain each particular cross. Once all 12 crosses have been collected, Jean must battle a rather surprising final boss.

Locomalito created the game during a vacation in southern France and styled it after the regions and sights he saw during day trips.

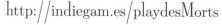

http://indiegam.es/playdesMorts

Sombreros

Dustin Gunn

Sombreros follows the story of a Mexican gunslinger who is on a mission to retrieve a number of sombreros that have been stolen by some nasty fellows. Upon taking to the streets, you must gun down anyone who opposes you and overtake the thieves in question.

The protagonist can fire his weapon rapidly and infinitely, which helps in taking on the waves of enemies. Even with this ability, *Sombreros* is fiendishly difficult, but fortunately the hero has another trick up his sleeve—pressing the C key will allow you to stop time so that your gunslinger can aim at the baddies and unleash bullet fury to take them all down in one fell swoop. There are also a number of duels along the way, during which you must shoot your opponents before they hit you.

Sombreros was created for the Action 52 Owns remake challenge. Another game called *Sombreros* also appeared on an unlicensed multicart collection for the NES and Genesis.

http://indiegam.es/playSombreros

UFO on Tape

Nicolai Troshinsky

The truth is out there! *UFO on Tape* puts you in the role of one lucky guy who has managed to spot a UFO. Fortunately, he's got his trusty (and very shaky) camcorder on hand to film the evidence.

As the flying saucer zooms around the sky, you'll need to use the mouse as if you were aiming a camcorder to keep the UFO in focus. Over time the view zooms in, and obstructions such as buildings and flocks of birds make it more difficult to follow the saucer. If the UFO moves out of range, the battery life on the camera will start to drop—and when it drops too low, the camcorder dies.

UFO on Tape was developed for an Experimental Gameplay competition with the theme "Zero Button." Indeed, the game is quite unique in that it uses no buttons on either your mouse or keyboard and instead relies solely on your mouse movements.

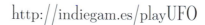

http://indiegam.es/playUFO

Privates

Zombie Cow Studios

When British television broadcaster Channel 4 asked Zombie Cow Studios to develop an educational game about sex, it's unlikely they had any idea what they were letting themselves in for. *Privates* was the result, and it's not exactly your average video game.

Privates puts you in control of a tiny army of condom-hatted soldiers as they venture into the orifices of the human body, killing STDs and dodging swarms of sperm. Each level explores a different part of the body and highlights the various sexually transmitted infections that can fester, along with information about their symptoms and treatments. The story is told from a very silly angle in the hope of appealing to teenagers, with voice acting that revels in the rude scenarios.

Originally, *Privates* was to be released on both PC and the Xbox 360, but after the PC release, Zombie Cow Studios was advised by Microsoft that the game would not be approved for release on the Xbox 360 due to the "strong sexual content."

http://indiegam.es/playPrivates

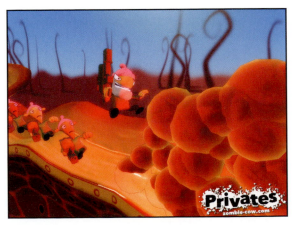

Mondo Medicals

Jonatan "Cactus" Söderström

Mondo Medicals is a twisted first-person puzzle game that will mess with your perception. You are a scientist who wants to join a team that's looking for a cure for cancer, but the initiation process into this particular team is rather odd.

On each level, you're tasked with finding the exit in a monochromatic, very creepy maze. Hints about how to complete the level are provided, but it's usually best to ignore them and attempt to break the rules—otherwise you may well find yourself walking around in circles. After you find each door, you'll be treated to a cutscene in which a strange man will shout bizarre anecdotes and make very unsettling noises.

Mondo Medicals was developed for a TIGSource contest with the theme "B-Games" (the theme celebrated "bad games with some great person-alities"). Spurred on by the positive response to his game, "Cactus" went on to create the sequel *Mondo Agency*, which is also very much worth playing.

http://indiegam.es/playmondo

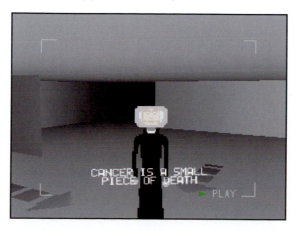

Man Enough

Daniel Remar and Erik Sjöstrand

Why play one game when you can play four games at once? In *Man Enough,* there are four completely different games all running at the same time and you must use the arrow keys and the space bar to beat each simultaneously.

The four games are a simple space shooter, a coin-collecting minigame, a Game & Watch style platformer, and a "bromancing" simulator. Every time you fail in one of the games, your total number of lives is reduced, until you've completely run out. A humorous song plays throughout, with lyrics that talk about each of the games and then tell you to "be a man" while displaying a picture of a popular male figure.

Man Enough was developed over the course of 36 hours at a game jam known as No More Sweden, where Swedish game developers get together for a weekend of co-operative game development.

http://indiegam.es/playManEnough

Shoot First

Beau Blyth

Shoot First is a retro-styled dungeon crawler with randomly generated levels. Players try to reach as low a floor as possible while blasting their way through hordes of tough enemies and looking for damsels in distress.

Along the way, you'll encounter special trap rooms with crushing boulders and moving walls, over-powered baddies that you'll want to run away from, and AI companions who will help you out in defeating the nasties. There are a variety of different weapons to find, and it's essential that you grab a more powerful blaster before venturing farther into the cave as some of the enemies that come later are extremely strong.

The game can also be experienced in two-player co-operative mode, which adds an extra element of fun. If you're connected to the Internet, your high scores will be uploaded and you'll be able to compare your efforts to those of other players around the world.

http://indiegam.es/playShootFirst

Desktop Dungeons

QCF Design

Desktop Dungeons is a puzzle-based RPG in which you must consider each move carefully so that you can slay every enemy in a randomly-generated dungeon. Starting at level one, the idea is to defeat low-level baddies to gain experience so that you can work your way up to the almighty boss battle.

There's a puzzle element that comes from being able to tackle the fights in whichever order you prefer. Exploring areas in the dungeon that you haven't already covered replenishes your health, as does leveling up—therefore, you can attack an enemy, move deeper into the level to gain extra HP, then go back and finish him off. There are also a variety of collectables to find, magic powers to experiment with, and gods to worship.

At the time of writing, the game is still early in development, although still very playable. Developer Rodain Joubert uploads each new version as he adds more races, classes, and game modes. A commercial version of the game is also in development.

http://indiegam.es/playDD

Dubloon

Greg "Banov" Lobanov

Dubloon is a pirating adventure that mixes RPG and point-and-click elements together. You play a young pirate who stumbles upon a great treasure chest full of gold while on a robbery mission, only to be captured and thrown into a cell.

This isn't enough to stop the anti-hero, however; he decides to get a crew together and find the treasure once again. Fights play out in classic turn-based RPG style; each character has special abilities, and players allocate stats to each of their team members. The game is gloriously long, with many hours of exploring and a great story to boot.

Dubloon was in development for more than a year, and was featured on both YoYo Games and GameJolt when it was released. A deluxe CD edition of the game is available from "Banov's" site for anyone who donates $15 or more.

http://indiegam.es/playDubloon

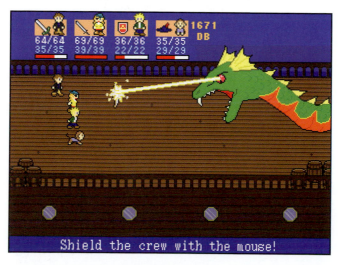

Shield the crew with the mouse!

The Life of a Pacifist

Selina "Bento Smile" Dean

The Life Of A Pacifist Is Often Fraught With Conflict (the game's full name) is a short visual novel with humorous dialogue. You are part of a game development team that has come together to discuss its latest project.

Unfortunately, you don't exactly agree with the ideas and methods of your fellow team members and it's eating away at you. Should you mention that you're not comfortable with the direction in which development is heading, or do you keep your mouth shut and just earn your keep? The script is quite dark at times as conflict ensues between you and your colleagues, and it serves as an inside look into the mainstream video game industry.

"Bento Smile" is well-known in the indie community for her tongue-in-cheek visual novels. Other of her releases that are worth checking out include *Air Pressure* and *Enemy of the Solid State*.

http://indiegam.es/playPacifist

Within a Deep Forest

Nicklas "Nifflas" Nygren

The evil Dr. Cliché wants to destroy the world by building an ice bomb that will freeze the land and everything in it. But his first attempt is a failure, resulting in the creation of a strange bouncy blue ball that's an unlikely but formidable hero.

Unfortunately, the second attempt goes off without a hitch and Dr. Cliché is on the verge of setting the bomb off. Players take control of the blue hero ball and begin an epic journey packed with clever platforming puzzles and plenty of exploration. You'll meet numerous allies along the way who will provide you with new powers, allowing your ball to bounce higher and even fly. These special abilities will be needed for traversing the trickier puzzles.

There are also hidden minigames to be found within the forest, and, once they're unlocked, they can be played via a separate executable.

http://indiegam.es/playWADF

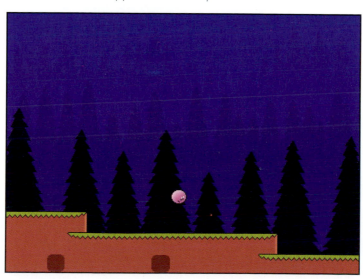

Hero Core

Daniel Remar

Hero Core puts you in the role of Flip Hero on his quest to destroy the evil Cruiser Tetron. It's a Metroid-style exploration shooter with lots of upgrades and numerous hidden secrets to find.

The twist is that the final boss is available from the very beginning and you can choose to fight it whenever you want—however, it would be very unwise to head straight in, as Cruiser Tetron would destroy you in seconds. Instead, you should explore the surrounding areas, finding as many weapons and health and armour upgrades as possible, so that you will actually stand a chance against the beast. *Hero Core* also features secondary missions to complete. The whole game takes about two hours to explore fully.

Hero Core is a sequel to one of Daniel's earlier releases, *Hero*, which is also available for free download. The full 28-minute long *Hero Core* chiptune soundtrack by Brother Android is also free.

http://indiegam.es/playHeroCore

Façade

Michael Mateas and Andrew Stern

When an old friend invites you over for cocktails with him and his wife at their swanky city apartment, how could you possibly refuse? However, it soon becomes apparent that *Façade* is going to throw a lot more than simply drinks and pleasant conversation your way.

Grace and Trip are in the middle of a relationship breakdown, and when you arrive, it isn't long before the tension bubbles over. As the couple argue, you can intervene and get involved by interacting with them and typing out full sentences via your keyboard. There is great voice acting throughout, and both characters will react to everything you type. There's even a list of popular names to choose from by which Grace and Trip can address you.

Depending on how you handle the situation, there are multiple endings to be found. Will you save their marriage, or push them even further apart?

http://indiegam.es/playFacade

Action Fist

Beau Blyth

In the style of a retro side-scrolling shooter, *Action Fist* tells the tale of a man who is out for revenge after having his favourite scarf stolen. One or two players can blast through a series of tricky levels, which feature a profusion of unlockables and power-ups.

Gameplay includes hectic driving sections, acrobatics ranging from double jumps to wall kicks, and epic boss fights. Specific-coloured lasers are available later in the game to inflict greater damage against enemies. Players can find an array of powerful weapons and upgrades throughout play, and if you try the more difficult settings you'll unlock new characters and features.

Action Fist was heavily inspired by Sega Genesis/Mega Drive shooter *Gunstar Heroes*—in fact, the weapon-combo system in Beau's blaster is nearly identical to that of the classic offering.

http://indiegam.es/playActionFist

They Need To Be Fed

Jesse Venbrux

Developed in the space of a week for the YoYo Games Design-a-Handheld competition—and taking home first place and a cool $1,000—*They Need To Be Fed* is a gravity-based platformer about getting yourself eaten by huge blobs with ferocious appetites.

The hero can jump between platforms, each of which has its own centre of gravity. This means that his movement is constantly changing depending on whichever platform he is closest to. At the end of each level, there is a huge monster with big teeth ready to gobble the protagonist up, and allowing it to do so is the key to completing the game. Diamonds must also be collected along the way to unlock new worlds.

After winning the YoYo Games contest, Jesse began helping YoYo Games port its popular Game Maker development tools to PSP and the iPhone, with the goal of bringing games like *They Need To Be Fed* to other platforms. Since then, the game has been released on the iPhone (with an additional world to explore!).

http://indiegam.es/playTNTBF

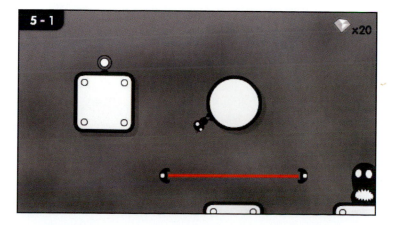

Spelunky

Derek Yu

Spelunky is a side-scrolling dungeon crawler that becomes more and more rewarding the longer you play it. Each playthrough is different, as the level layout, enemy placement, and items that are up for grabs are all randomly generated.

Players take control of a short but nimble adventurer. Armed with bombs, ropes, and a whip, he must traverse a series of randomly-generated caves, collecting loot and saving damsels in distress. At first, it's difficult to make progress in *Spelunky* as there are no save points and certain traps will kill you instantly. However, the experience becomes more rewarding as you venture farther into the caves and discover new items, weapons, and enemies.

Due to the success of the PC version of *Spelunky*, an Xbox Live Arcade edition has gone into development; the new commercial version will feature additional game modes, high resolution comic-like visuals, and a chiptune soundtrack.

http://indiegam.es/playSpelunky

Girlfriend vs. Boyfriend

Shaun Pauley

In *Girlfriend vs. Boyfriend*, you play a guy who is in serious trouble with his girlfriend for eyeballing another woman. She proceeds to chase you, throwing all sorts of objects your way, including fruit, animals, and tables.

The game is controlled with a single button; holding the button down causes the protagonist to stop and block whatever is hurtling his way, and letting go makes him run. There are things to help our hero, like food to give him health and bicycles to let him ride away from his pursuer. Do not let the girlfriend catch up with you—she'll hit you with a "Punishment" move and you'll lose a life.

The game was created for a GAMMA IV competition that didn't require sound, as the winners were to be exhibited on a noisy showroom floor—consequently, the game doesn't feature any sound or music.

http://indiegam.es/playGvB

Go! Underground

Dot Zo Games

Go! Underground (or *Journey to the Center of the Earth*) takes a player into the depths of the Earth to explore subterranean environments and collect relics. A treasure map gives hints as to the location of each relic, and your task is to unlock a variety of paths and find all 40.

Our hero is armed with an unlimited supply of bombs that can be used to take out enemies and launch him to greater heights. Keys must be collected to open locked doors and pathways and to unlock treasure chests so that you can accumulate relics. The entire width of the playing area is displayed at all times, although as the hero moves deeper underground the screen will scroll to reveal the new areas below.

The game was quite the underground hit (excuse the pun!) thanks to its unique zoomed-out graphical style, and was one of Gamasutra's Top 10 Indie Games of 2009.

http://indiegam.es/playUnderground

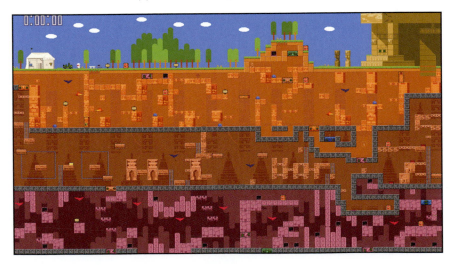

Dungeons of Fayte

Brent Ellison

Dungeons of Fayte is a dungeon crawler for one to four players with enough content to keep either a single player or a group of friends going for a good while. The Bone Lord, ruler of the Underworld, is planning an attack and the heroes need to train in various dungeons before taking the Bone Lord and his cronies on.

During play, an old man gives humorous tips on how to stay alive, and random occurrences mean that the game has lots of replay value. You and your friends can venture into town between dungeons to hone your skills—perhaps by learning new moves at the barracks, taking money from the dead in the graveyard, or buying new weapons at the supply shop.

Dungeons of Fayte was developed for the TIGSource Assemblee competition, which had designers create graphics, sounds, and music that developers could then pick from to use for their games. Assets for this game came from designers Oddball, Oryx, Geese, Atuun, Jorge Boscan, Shaktool, Stian Stark, Craig Stern, JRHill, Patrick Alexander, Synnah, Wyvern, Stevobread, and Shackles.

http://indiegam.es/playFayte

Psychosomnium

Jonatan "Cactus" Söderström

Psychosomnium is a short and very quirky platformer set in the dream of protagonist Jimmy. There are plenty of situations where continuing on appears impossible, yet there is always a method for reaching the next screen.

The game attempts to capture the feelings and logic of a dream, with strange doings and dialogue that you'd never have in real life. The puzzles feel completely illogical yet give the sense that, if this were a dream, you'd solve them in an instant. Situations change constantly—again, as in a dream—and characters give way to other characters as a matter of course.

Developed over three days, *Psychosomnium* features a trippy colour scheme, odd characters, and very strange dialogue, epitomising the type of gaming experience for which developer "Cactus" is best known.

http://indiegam.es/playPsycho

Seiklus

clysm

Seiklus (the Estonian word for "adventure") is a platforming adventure game that was released back in 2003. Players navigate a series of strange environments in an unknown world, collecting floating wisps and discovering secret areas along the way.

The intro shows a white figure being knocked off a cliff by a falling meteor, but since the game doesn't feature any storytelling or dialogue, players can make up their own plots. There are no weapons, violence, or death in the game, and your few opponents will only knock you back. If you collect all the wisps, you'll open up a final bonus area; once you've completed that, you'll be able to see the video that ends the game.

Seiklus has had a huge impact on many indie developers—inspiring the likes of "Nifflas" and Matt Thorson—and has also helped to promote the now-popular Game Maker development tools.

http://indiegam.es/playSeiklus

Hydorah

Locomalito

Hydorah is a tough horizontal shooter that harks back to the challenge levels of shooters from the late '80s. Players take on the role of a crack-shot space pilot who travels from planet to planet battling hordes of evil Meroptians.

As enemies are destroyed, you collect power-ups that will strengthen your ship and provide extra firepower. There are 16 levels to blast your way through, but don't expect to reach the last level for a good few hours as you'll most likely become a cropper a number of times before then. *Hydorah* is a seriously difficult game, and you'll need lots of practice to beat it. The game only provides you with three saves—after that, you're forced to start from the beginning.

As with many of the classic side-scrolling shooters of old, *Hydorah* features plenty of big boss battles, along with a great finger-tapping soundtrack and gorgeous pixelated visuals.

http://indiegam.es/playHydorah

The Graveyard

Tale of Tales

Tale of Tales describes *The Graveyard* as "more like an explorable painting than an actual game," and it's not difficult to see why. You are an old lady as she hobbles slowly through a monochrome graveyard.

There is only a single path to walk down, and the woman is limited to sitting down on a bench at the end of the path, standing back up again, and walking back out of the graveyard. The idea behind the experience is to allow the player to see the world through the eyes of an elderly person by means of the extremely slow movements and aimless roaming, yet still feel the emotion in what, at first glance, appears to be rather dull action.

There is also a commercial version of *The Graveyard*, which adds an extra dimension to the experience—the possibility of death. In this version, the woman drifts into dreams if she sits on the bench and may pass away.

http://indiegam.es/playGraveyard

5 Days A Stranger

Ben "Yahtzee" Croshaw

5 Days A Stranger is a horror adventure game developed by Ben "Yahtzee" Croshaw, best known as the creator and voice of the controversial Internet review series *Zero Punctuation*. You play Trilby, a cat burglar who is attempting to loot a country manor. The story is told through some tense—and sometimes humorous—dialogue.

Trilby realises that the manor is not all that it appears to be while he's trying to escape, and some of the people he's trapped in the house with are murdered. You'll need to solve a lot of puzzles if you want Trilby to leave the house alive, and you should save frequently as there are many points at which you can die in this story.

The game was developed in 2003 using Adventure Game Studio tools, and it won an incredible five Adventure Game Studio awards that year. A sequel called *7 Days A Skeptic* was later released.

http://indiegam.es/play5Days

And Everything Started To Fall

Andújar "Alexitrón" González

And Everything Started To Fall is a simple platformer about life and death. The protagonist starts at the bottom as a child and slowly works his way up to the top, passing through each stage of his life along the way.

The hero passes numerous greyed-out scenes, which show events that have occurred in his life. He gets to the next stage at intervals you'd expect; for example, reaching school advances him from a baby to a child, and progressing to work sees him become an adult. Eventually, the inevitable end is reached. Ambiguous metaphors are plentiful; for instance, do the pools of water filled with cash mean that he is swimming in money, or drowning in debt?

The game was developed for an Experimental Gameplay Project competition with the theme "Art," and was the winner of the contest.

http://indiegam.es/playAESTF

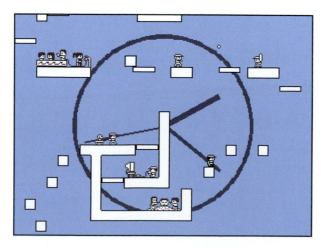

Lyle in Cube Sector

"Bogosoft"

Lyle in Cube Sector tells the story of one man's journey to retrieve his beloved cat from an unnamed thief. Since Lyle does not possess the powers required to follow the culprit, he must first explore the Cube Sector, where he dodges villains while he collects the necessary abilities.

The game is rather difficult, especially at the beginning when Lyle has no way to defend himself against attacks and must instead manoeuvre around his opponents until he has what he needs to fight back. The level layout and visual style are very reminiscent of the classic SNES-era Metroid series, with pathways opening up once you have collected the necessary powers. As the game's name suggests, cubes play a big part in the gameplay and Lyle is eventually able to use a variety of blocks to his advantage.

The entire game was developed over the course of five months. The name comes from a children's book that developer "Bogosoft" read when he was young called *Lyle, Lyle, Crocodile.*

http://indiegam.es/playLyle

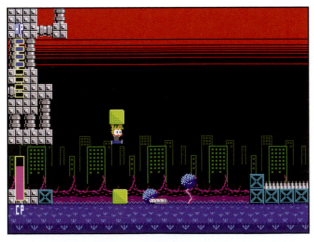

Illuminator

Logan Ames

Armed with just a flashlight, a boy sets out to save his sister from a band of nasty ghouls who have the ability to tear through the fabric of space and who travel from house to house in the dead of night.

Fortunately for our hero, the ghosties are susceptible to bright light and will burn up on the spot if exposed to it. The boy must travel through his neighbourhood, shining his torch to light the way and to expose the ghosts. The batteries in his flashlight aren't so great and will only power the light for a few seconds, but energy flows back when he turns the light off. Correctly balancing use of the torch with charging the batteries will make the difference between finding your sister and being dragged away yourself!

Illuminator is a remake of a game that had the same name and was part of a SNES multicart collection called Action 52. The game was created as part of the Action 52 Owns project that was started by TIGSource members.

http://indiegam.es/playIlluminator

An Untitled Story

Matt Thorson

An Untitled Story follows an egg's adventures after it has rolled out of its nest and starts to explore its huge world. Throughout play, the mysterious setting and the egg's enemies reveal its story.

The egg encounters a variety of creative boss battles and has plenty of opportunities to collect power-ups and earn special abilities like the double jump, the fire shot, and the dive bomb. The environments in *An Untitled Story* are simple but fun, with some great level design on offer. At the beginning, you're not given much information about your journey, but the story gradually comes to light through cutscenes. Multiple difficulty settings accommodate a wide range of players.

A two-player competitive mode is available in addition to the lengthy single-player story, and Heist mode features two friends stealing bags of money from each other in a variety of arenas.

http://indiegam.es/playUntitled

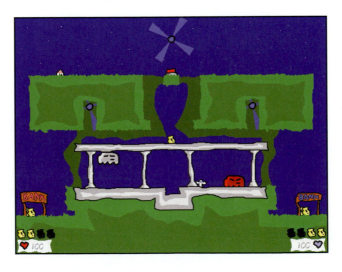

Knight of the Living Dead

Pistachio Productions

Camelot is being overrun by zombie knights, and only the brave Sir Galahad can hold them back and restore peace to the kingdom. *Knight of the Living Dead* is an action-packed arena slasher with constant waves of the undead that need to be slayed quickly.

As Galahad cuts the zombies down with his blade, he earns a range of magical powers that will allow him to hold back the masses more easily. Gradually he'll level up, which lets players boost their stats and upgrade their abilities. Enemies get more powerful and come in larger groups with each new wave, but Galahad's powers also get stronger and he's able to mow down hundreds of zombies at a time. Players can even choose to increase the number of zombies in a wave, which makes the waves more dangerous but also allows for faster completion times.

There are two different campaigns to play through, and online leaderboards track the best weekly and overall times.

http://indiegam.es/playKOTLD

Classic Night

YoungWon "Akarolls" Jo

The moon wants to be as bright as the sun, so it hires a skeleton called Harigol to help fulfil this dream. *Classic Night* is a strategy game with construction elements that follows Harigol as he goes about his assignment.

Harigol must collect light from plants that are growing on the moon and use them to build streetlights. He can walk up walls and on to the ceiling of the level—the camera will simply rotate to follow his movements. Once the main elements are explained, extra hindrances are introduced to keep you on your toes, like small creatures called Siros who steal any light they come across, and a nasty monster called Crazy Rabbit who will chase you around the level.

Unfortunately, a thief broke into the developer's house and stole the computer that contained the game's source code before *Classic Night* was finished. Therefore, the experience is not complete and ends rather abruptly.

http://indiegam.es/playClassicNight

Streemerz

Arthur "Mr. Podunkian" Lee

Sent into the belly of a floating fortress, operative Joe has his mission—find the Tiger Army's top-secret weapon and destroy it. However, Joe cannot jump and so must scale the fortress using his special grappling hook-style streamers, which can only be fired at a 45-degree angle.

With the streamers, Joe can launch himself over obstacles and stick to walls and ceilings if he fires them fast enough. As he penetrates the heart of the enemy base, there are plenty of hazards and enemies to dodge, including clowns throwing pies, random firetraps, and "Master Y's balls." The going can get pretty tough later on, but fortunately there are a multitude of checkpoints along the way so you're never sent too far back.

The game was developed for the Action 52 Owns remake project, which developer Arthur himself set up. Each participant was tasked with remaking a game from the infamous Action 52 NES multicart, and *Streemerz* is based on an Action 52 game of the same name.

http://indiegam.es/playStreemerz

The Soul of Dracula

Bunaguchi

The Soul of Dracula is a dark Japanese platformer heavily inspired by the classic *Castlevania* series. A vampire hunter journeys to the Dark Prince's castle armed with a rather familiar whip, which he can use to cut down the skeletons, bats, and ghouls that cross his path.

If you're a big fan of the *Castlevania* games from the '80s and '90s, then this game is for you, with tough enemies to defeat and a number of great boss-battle encounters (like the fights against Death and the Count). The hero will find numerous special weapons and projectiles along the way to aid him in his quest, and there are many different twists and turns to keep the story interesting.

The download page is in Japanese but the game itself is in English. There's also a level-select option that allows you to quit the game at any point and resume play from that point later on.

http://indiegam.es/playDracula

Nudo

Ben Esposito and Manuel Pardo

Developers Ben Esposito and Manuel Pardo describe *Nudo* as "a platformer on top of a rubik's cube," which turns out to be a rather apt description. You reach the goal on each level by shifting blocks around and creating platforms to jump across.

There are two twists: you can only move the column of blocks you're standing on, and columns can only move up and down. You'll have to be creative to work around these limitations so that you can arrange the blocks to your advantage, and you may have to press buttons or slide blocks into specific positions before the exit will appear. There are quite a variety of levels, which range from simple, uncluttered areas to those that are extremely complex and messy.

Ben Esposito was an intern with Dejobaan Games (the developer of *Aaaaa!— A Reckless Disregard for Gravity*) and quipped "after seeing what it's like to make games with no money and no air conditioning, I decided to start doing it myself."

http://indiegam.es/playNudo

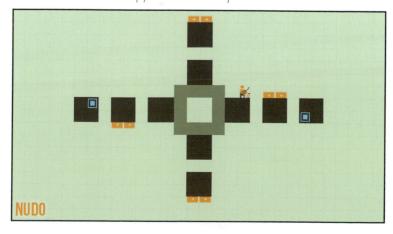

The Hive

Vanni del Moral

The mining town of Redforest Mountain is a serene and well-regarded community in the Northwest—that is, until a horrible secret about the town is revealed: hundreds of people have been disappearing from the town without a trace. Eventually, the town is abandoned and sealed off.

Alex Rig, a reporter for the *Bulletin Times*, receives an anonymous tip that something is going on in the town and sets off to investigate. He soon finds more than he bargained for in the form of a strange underground base full of armed soldiers, hostages, and monsters. Fortunately, Alex can climb through vents to navigate around danger, use his Taser to disable his attackers, and pick up a variety of health and weapon upgrades to help him complete his investigation.

The Hive was developed for a YoYo Games competition with the theme "Discovery" and won first prize, a $1,000 pot.

http://indiegam.es/playHive

Ninja Senki

Jonathan Lavigne

Ninja Senki is a retro-styled platformer that takes inspiration from a classic Japanese NES game called *Ninja Jajamaru-Kun*. You take control of Hayate, a ninja who sets out to avenge the death of the princess Kinuhime.

Hayate can double jump and throw shurikens to cut his enemies down. The action feels very reminiscent of platformers from the late '80s, as the ninja must make tight, timed jumps and be ready to throw those shurikens the moment his feet touch the ground. There are a variety of bad guys, each with their own particular attack patterns, and enough falling platform sections to have you moving swiftly yet precisely along.

The game has 16 levels, multiple endings, and a continue system that lets you carry on even after you've run out of lives. Note that it does not come with a save feature; therefore, you'll need to complete your playthrough in one sitting.

http://indiegam.es/playNinjaSenki

Frogatto & Friends

Lost Pixel

Frogatto is a gorgeous platformer that feels like a cross between *Rayman* and *Kirby*. Frogatto is a lazy frog who sets off to town in search of a job, but soon discovers that there is trouble afoot.

Frogatto can hop between platforms, kick his way up tight platforming sections, and spring from walls. He can also use his long tongue to pull a bad guy into his mouth and then spit him back out, which allows Frogatto to disable his opponent for a few seconds or even knock one enemy into another. Coins are scattered around each area, which can be spent on upgrades to help Frogatto progress. There are a variety of fun and interesting characters to meet along the way, and beautiful pixel-art foregrounds and backdrops throughout.

In addition to the free PC and Mac versions of *Frogatto & Friends*, there is also a commercial iPhone edition available for download.

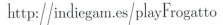

http://indiegam.es/playFrogatto

Flood the Chamber

Matt Scorah

A prisoner has escaped from solitary confinement and is trying to escape from prison. As he runs off towards the exit, a guard shouts "Flood the chamber!" and water begins to rise, leaving the rogue in quite a predicament.

Even without a time limit, *Flood the Chamber* would be tough, but the never-ending threat of the water adds even more tension to the gameplay. As you proceed through the levels, there are precision jumps to make and timing is the key to success—many of the jumps aren't too difficult, but the water is constantly pressuring you by making even simple tasks much more taxing. The prisoner will regenerate at the most recent checkpoint if he's killed by a saw or a spike, but if the water catches up to him, it's game over.

Flood the Chamber was developed for the Gamejolt Rogue contest and took home third prize.

http://indiegam.es/playFlood

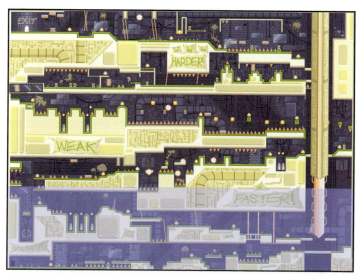

Darkfate

Kevin "Twiner" Soulas

Darkfate is an exploration platformer that follows Chris Freeman, a man whose memory has failed him. He has no idea why he's wandering around a snowy mountainside in freezing weather and decides to venture into nearby caves to seek out answers. During his odyssey, he keeps a record of his thoughts in a journal.

After only a short while, Chris finds out how he got where he is, and when he does, the story takes a bizarre and twisted turn. Throughout play, Chris continues to remember events from his past and slowly he pieces together what he has seen. If Chris falls down a hole or drops too far, his journey will end, but the game will also tell you that this is not his destiny and places him back in the last area he was in.

The game was developed for the Clickteam and GameBuilder 2010 Twenty Event competition, which restricted the number of lines of code participants could use to build their games. *Darkfate* placed second in the contest.

http://indiegam.es/playDarkfate

TowerClimb

Davioware

Developed for the Gamejolt Rogue contest (in which it placed second), *TowerClimb* is a procedurally-generated platformer about a tower that no one has ever managed to scale all the way to the top. Will you be its next victim, or will you overcome all obstacles and emerge victorious?

The simple answer is that you will die, as the tower is in fact endless—however, you'll also have an extremely good time on the way up. The hero can latch onto walls and ceilings to elude enemies and avoid pits of deadly spikes, and also has access to a number of special potions and berries that can be used to gain extra strength (although it's not a good idea to eat too many berries!). The specifics of the game change each time you play so replays are fun and give you a chance to beat your previous best, since your highest climb is always recorded.

At the time of writing, Davioware was adding more content and ideas to update the game and expand on its original concept.

http://indiegam.es/playTowerClimb

Under the Garden

Paul Greasley

A terrible storm is blowing in, and its harsh winds have wrecked your little house. *Under the Garden* is a survival exploration game, and your goal is to find supplies in the wilderness then build your house back up in whatever way you like.

You begin with an axe that can be used to chop down trees to feed your fire, which keeps you alive. Outside the comfort of your shelter, the rain beats down hard, and your health deteriorates slowly whenever you're outdoors. But as you venture farther from your home, you'll also find more tools for interacting with the landscape, and slowly but surely find pieces to attach to your abode. These pieces can be placed however you like, so building up your house is a very enjoyable, sandbox-style experience.

Under the Garden was developed for the TIGSource A Game Its Cover competition and won first place. A complex level editor also comes with the game, allowing you to create your own worlds.

http://indiegam.es/playGarden

Momodora

Guilherme "rdein" Martins

The people of Koho have a strange and unsettling ritual that they believe makes the world a better place: they believe that if maidens are sacrificed, the world will be re-created and life will improve.

As you'd expect, not everyone is happy with this ritual. An orphan girl who lost her mother to this superstition enters a dangerous labyrinth in search of a treasure that might be able to bring her mother back to life. As she battles her way through numerous tough platforming areas, Isadora can swipe at and destroy enemies with a magic leaf. She'll also find additional weapons throughout the game that can be switched back and forth to fit each situation.

Momodora's graphical style and gameplay was heavily inspired by the highly regarded indie game *Cave Story*, as well as by a variety of other mainstream titles, including the likes of *Mega Man*, *Metal Slug* and *The Legend of Zelda*.

http://indiegam.es/playMomodora

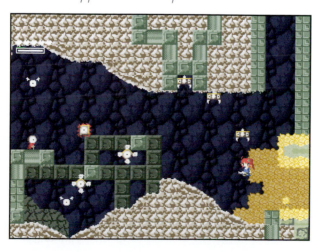

Strange Adventures in Infinite Space

Digital Eel

Strange Adventures in Infinite Space provides brief voyages with infinite possibilities in the depths of space. As the governments of the Glory system argue over who owns the surrounding planets, you set out to take all the resources and wealth for yourself.

The positioning of the planets, stars, enemies, and black holes is completely random each time you play, as are the events that occur and the items, ship upgrades, and allies you can find. Hence, every new game of *Strange Adventures* is different, providing oodles of replay value. With ten years to explore the solar system, you can blast off to any planet you like, fighting alien races and stealing treasure. Games only last around ten minutes, so whether you're looking for a quick flight of fancy or a longer experience, this game can provide both.

A commercial sequel to *Strange Adventures* called *Weird Worlds: Return to Infinite Space* is also available for both the PC and the iPad.

http://indiegam.es/playInfiniteSpace

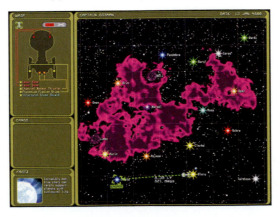

Punishment

Mark "messhof" Essen

If you get frustrated easily, it would probably be best to steer clear of "messhof's" *Punishment*. It's a simple platformer turned very nasty, with screen-rotation and control-flipping features designed to totally disorient you during play.

For starters, the level rotates left or right depending on which direction you're moving as you climb the tower. There are also spinning eyeballs that turn the screen if you touch them, so you may find yourself playing a completely upside-down level. If that isn't enough, there are flashing donkeys that will flip your controls so that left is right and right is left. All the while, strange images fade in and out in the background as you progress, and the music gets faster to build the tension. Make just one false move and you may fall all the way to the bottom.

An encouraging response from the indie community inspired developer Mark Essen to create a sequel, *Punishment 2: The Punishing*, which plays in a similar fashion.

http://indiegam.es/playpunishment

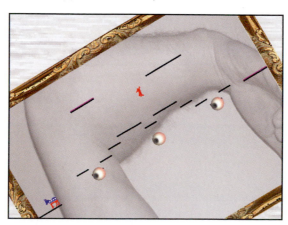

Passage

Jason Rohrer

Described as an "art game," *Passage* tells the story of a man's journey through life. As you move the protagonist to the right, he proceeds through each stage of his existence until he eventually grows old and dies.

Near the beginning of his journey, he passes a girl who will follow him if he gets close to her. Bring the girl with you, however, and you will no longer be able to grab some of the treasure chests that are scattered around the world. Yet when you reach the end of the game, your score fades away to nothing, symbolizing the balance of money and love—surely it's more important to spend your life with someone you love than to chase riches that, on your deathbed, will have no meaning?

Passage is just one of the games developed by Jason Rohrer, who is recognised as one of the key developers driving the art game scene forward.

http://indiegam.es/playPassage

Noitu Love

Joakim "konjak" Sandberg

An organisation known as The Peacekeeper's League keeps war at bay in the year 2188. Yet even with its protection, the world is not safe—the evil professor Darnacus Damnation has unleashed his army of Grinning Darns to wreak havoc.

Fortunately, there is one hope for the people of the world: Noitu Love, a young boy with extraordinary fighting abilities. You'll revel in the button-mashing, beat-'em-up action as, led by his teammate Lori, Noitu sets out to destroy the Grinning Darns. Later on you'll discover machines that can turn Noitu into an animal, allowing him to access areas that he couldn't earlier in the game. The pixel art in this game is lovely, the level design is slick and enjoyable, and the boss battles are particularly clever.

A commercial sequel that focuses more on mouse gesturing to achieve special moves is also available. *Noitu Love 2: Devolution* is set 100 years after the events of the original game, and once again puts players up against the evil Darnacus Damnation as he resurrects his Darn army.

http://indiegam.es/playNoituLove

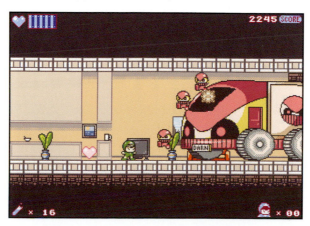

Mighty Jill Off

Anna "Dessgeega" Anthropy

Jill has been kicked to the bottom of the tower by her queen, and must now jump back up to the top again. Of course, it's not that simple with spikes, fire, and the other traps that will knock Jill back down again if she's not careful.

You'll find that the jumping controls are rather unique and tricky to master, making her ascent even more difficult. Pressing the Z key causes Jill to leap into the air at full speed; tapping it again while she's airborne allows her to stop in mid-jump and fall back down again. If you tap Z rapidly as she drops, you'll slow down her descent. You'll need to perfect these moves if you want to reach the top of the tower, since precision jumps and drops are required throughout the game.

Mighty Jill Off was inspired by the *Bomb Jack* arcade series from the '80s (the name comes from *Mighty Bomb Jack*, the second game). There's another tower to climb for any player who manages to complete the game in less than 12 minutes.

http://indiegam.es/playMJO

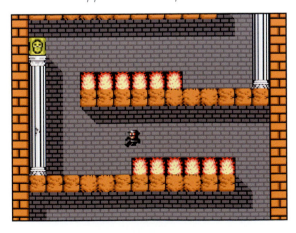

Aether

Edmund McMillen and Tyler Glaiel

Feeling lonely and desperate for a friend, a young boy goes off into the wilderness. He soon finds a strange space creature who offers him a ride on his back, and the duo set off into space to visit the surrounding planets, swinging from asteroids as they go.

In *Aether,* each planet has a secret and a puzzle to be solved, and since you're never directly told how to uncover each mystery, you must explore and experiment to figure things out. Your squid-like friend moves by grabbing clouds and space rocks with his long tongue, swinging to gain momentum, and launching himself upwards to grab onto something else. Every time that you solve a planet's conundrum, colour is restored to the land; by helping each planet's inhabitants, the boy and the creature go down in history as space-faring heroes.

Aether is a browser game that the developers describe as "an art game about personal childhood feelings and experiences." It's had over 1.5 million plays since its release in 2008.

http://indiegam.es/playAether

Destructivator

Pug Fugly Games

An evil genius called Zallagor has been secretly building up an army for decades, and has finally unleashed it on the world. The population of the planet is enslaved and there is only one hope: Destructivator, the ultimate soldier.

Similar in visual style to the 1983 Commodore game *Lode Runner, Destructivator* is a fast-paced blaster in which you must destroy every enemy on the screen in order to progress. The element of surprise will be your most powerful weapon—in order to prevail, you'll need to scramble onto platforms quickly and shoot all your opponents before they have a chance to fire off a bullet in your direction. Gradually, your enemies will become stronger, with much more deadly missiles that you'll have to dodge. Fortunately, the hero can be hit numerous times before dying and can also pick up health boxes along the way.

If you can blast your way through all 20 levels, you'll reach Zallagor's lair and be tasked with ridding the world of him once and for all.

http://indiegam.es/playDestructivator

Opera Omnia

Stephen "increpare" Lavelle

Looking for an experience that will really test your noggin? In *Opera Omnia,* you'll be challenged as you take on the role of a chief historian whose job is to input theories about past migration into the World History System.

You'll be given information about a particular era and will need to record migration routes by drawing lines between cities with your mouse. However, you'll also have to pay attention to the timeline at the bottom of the screen that stretches from the present into the past. As natural disasters such as famine occur, populations will move and you'll need to move the slider along to alter your migration paths accordingly. Later on in the game, the vibe becomes a little eerie as "the others"' are introduced into the story.

The game can be difficult to understand at first, especially since the timeline feels as though it's backwards. However, once you wrap your head around the idea that you are logging where migration routes end not where they begin, *Opera Omnia* will prove itself to be one of the more enjoyable puzzlers you can play.

http://indiegam.es/playOpera

Bonesaw

Kyle Pulver

The Bonesaw is the secret weapon of the Golden Knights, an ice hockey team named after its real-life counterpart at Clarkson University in New York. The day before a big game, an evil referee takes the whole team hostage, with the exception of a single player who must rescue them all.

The game consists of sections that blend platforming, puzzle, and beat-'em-up gameplay with a side of exploration. Players from opposing teams are positioned all over the place, and the hero must beat up every one to progress. He collects their blood to power up his ultimate weapon—the Bonesaw—which you can use to destroy hordes of your opponents in a single swipe by pressing the space bar.

There are special golden pucks on each level that can be difficult to find. Your progress through the *Bonesaw* world is tracked on a map like those used in the classic *Super Mario World* games.

http://indiegam.es/playBonesaw

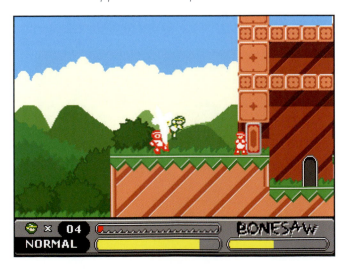

La-Mulana

GR3 Project

Legend tells of a land where the very first civilisation was formed—a people from whom the whole human race sprang. This land is called La-Mulana, and Professor Lemeza has finally found it after searching far and wide for many years.

La-Mulana is not your typical adventure platformer. Harking back to the days of tough and unrelenting gaming, the journey it features is a difficult one. Lemeza begins with a simple whip as his weapon, and must progress through a series of tombs full of nasty enemies who are tough to beat. Visuals are reminiscent of those from the old MSX home computers of the '80s. What makes *La-Mulana* so interesting is the non-linear pathways, which provide players with multiple ways to venture. The game, however, offers no clues as to which routes to take.

Although the game is in Japanese, there is an English translation patch available for download from Aeon Genesis. A version with updated graphics is currently in the works for the Nintendo Wii.

http://indiegam.es/playlamulana

Teppoman

"Ikiki"

Teppoman is a simple run 'n' gun platformer that stars a naked hero. Terrorists have taken a number of your fellow nudists hostage and your job is to bust in, take the enemies out, and free your unclothed friends.

The game doesn't try to throw any clever concepts your way, opting instead for an all-out blast fest with assorted weapons to find and lots of blood to be spilled. The game is in Japanese, but there is barely any dialogue involved. The only keys you'll need are the arrow keys to move, Shift to jump, Ctrl to use your weapons, and the down arrow to pick up any guns off the floor.

There is also an indirect sequel available. *Teppoman 2* puts you in control of a caped protagonist who enters a high-security fortress to take back his bananas. The sequel is far more technical than the original, as the hero has a number of special skills (including wall jumps, reverse jumps, and gliding) at his disposal.

http://indiegam.es/playTeppoman

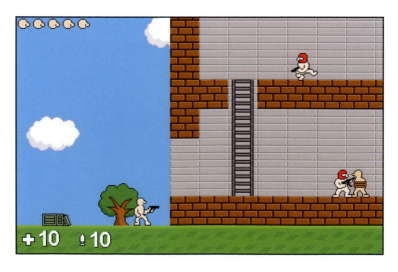

Barkley, Shut Up and Jam: Gaiden

Tales of Game's Studios

Barkley, Shut Up and Jam: Gaiden, Chapter 1 of the Hoopz Barkley SaGa (its full name) is a tongue-in-cheek RPG that acts as an unofficial sequel to the 1995 basketball game *Barkley Shut Up and Jam*. The game is set in a future where basketball has been outlawed after a "Chaos Dunk" killed millions of people.

The hero is real-life NBA star Charles Barkley, who the game has living in a post-apocalyptic "Neo New York" with his son. A second Chaos Dunk has killed all the inhabitants of another city and Barkley has been wrongly accused of the crime, so he must go into hiding until he can clear his name. The game features a whole host of real basketball players as characters, and frequently references the 1996 Warner Brothers film *Space Jam*. Battles occur in classic turn-based RPG style, and players will have the opportunity to meet up with a variety of teammates and accumulate an assortment of special abilities.

Even if you have no knowledge of basketball or its players, *Barkley, Shut Up and Jam: Gaiden* is still highly enjoyable, with a hilarious storyline throughout.

http://indiegam.es/playBarkley

Nanobots

Erin Robinson

Groovy Greg has created a bunch of tiny robots that have the ability to feel love. Unfortunately, there isn't much love involved at all—the bots argue constantly with each other. But it turns out that the evil Professor Killfun wants to smash them into pieces, and with the scrapheap looming, the six Nanobots finally start working together to escape from Killfun and help Greg complete his thesis.

The player controls each of the robots separately in classic point-and-click style, and each robot has its own special ability that must be used cooperatively with the other bots. For example, Hotbot can heat up the surrounding area, while Strongbot can lift heavy items. Throughout play, the Nanobots continue to irritate each other with hilarious exchanges.

With the success that *Nanobots* enjoyed, developer Erin Robinson decided to expand the concept, creating a paid, indirect sequel called *Puzzle Bots,* with a new set of robots and a whole lot of polish.

http://indiegam.es/playNanobots

Tombed

Anna "Dessgeega" Anthropy

If anyone can overcome the dangers hidden away in the tombs of Tamara-Kama and find the incredible treasures of legend, it must surely be brave explorer Danger Jane and her magnificent shovelling skills.

Jane starts digging for her life immediately upon entering the tombs, as a ceiling of spikes begins closing in. The floors are made up of coloured blocks that crumble and take all the adjacent matching colour chunks with them as she digs. The idea is to dig through the blocks to create a line of escape for Jane and allow her to move rapidly through the floor. Blocks will be removed from the spiked ceiling as well, depending on the colours it hits. All the colour coordination results in a game with a great combination of puzzles and fast-paced action that's loaded with close calls throughout.

Tombed was developed in two days for a Ludum Dare competition with the theme "Advancing Wall of Doom," hence the advancing and very deadly spikes.

http://indiegam.es/playTombed

I Was in the War

"Bisse"

I Was in the War is either a philosophical look at how war can escalate out of control or an action-packed—and rather distorted—arcade game that requires quick reactions and a steady hand. It all depends on your approach.

As your soldier storms the battlefield, he'll grow in size and make the enemy look very small, but if he stops for a moment, he'll begin to shrink again. There is no way to attack the opposing side, so instead you must either jump over them or flip over to the other side of the red walkway to advance. Over time, huge tanks and helicopters will come racing along and try to cut you down a notch or two.

The entire game was developed in just over three hours for a contest on The Poppenkast Forums with the theme "10800 Seconds" (exactly three hours).

http://indiegam.es/playIntheWar

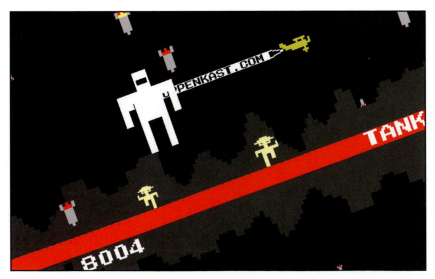

Flywrench

Mark "messhof" Essen

Flywrench is an arcade game with a seemingly simple premise that offers very challenging play. Like a manic flapping butterfly in space, Flywrench is on a mission to visit each planet in our solar system and must pass through various coloured gates on each level to reach his destinations.

Whenever Flywrench flaps his wings, his body turns from white to red. This movement is used not only to keep him aloft, but also to allow him to pass through the coloured gates, since he must be the correct colour in order to pass through each. He also has command of a roll move that will turn his body green so that he can pass through the green gates. Gates and objects of all other colours must be avoided.

Keeping Flywrench under control is a challenge, and later levels of the game are extremely difficult but ultimately rewarding. Developer Mark Essen is currently working on an expanded commercial version of the game.

http://indiegam.es/playFlywrench

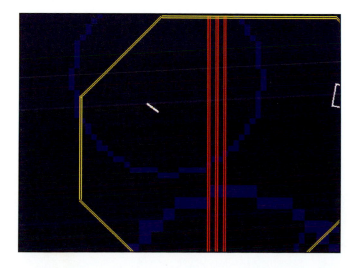

Part 2

Browser-Based Games

The next group of games are played via a web browser, and will usually require either the Flash or the Unity plug-in. Both can be installed on your computer with relative ease, and both are compatible with all the popular Internet browsers.

It doesn't matter whether you're using a PC or a Mac, as browser games can be played on both. The majority of browser games can be found on special game-hosting sites such as Kongregate, Newgrounds, and Armor Games, where players can earn special achievements and join in community discussions.

Hoshi Saga Ringo

Yoshio "Nekogames" Ishii

Hoshi Saga is a series of tricky puzzles from Japanese developer Yoshio Ishii. Individual games are comprised of a collection of "stages," each of which conceals a star. You either find the star or build it using each stage's available pieces.

Hoshi Saga Ringo is the fourth in the series, and the first to be in colour rather than in black and white. There are a total of 25 puzzles to solve: 16 can be tackled immediately, and the other 9 open up as you find stars. Difficulty ratings of levels are (of course!) given in stars and range from half a star (for simple puzzles) to five stars (for fiendishly difficult brain-teasers).

Compared to the rest of the series, *Hoshi Saga Ringo* is perhaps one of the easier collections and therefore a good starting point for investigating the *Hoshi Saga* series.

http://indiegam.es/playHoshiSaga

Garden Gnome Carnage

Daniel Remar

Garden Gnome Carnage is a Christmas miracle! You play a green-clothed elf with sunglasses who hates Christmas and wants to stop the rest of the elves from delivering presents and spreading cheer.

The best way to do this, of course, is to bungee-jump from the top of a building and slap all the elves off the sides as they attempt to scale the house and put presents down the chimney. Players control the direction of the swinging elf by moving the building (which is on wheels) left and right. Later on, sleighs fly in and try to land on the roof of your building and you need to beat them off, too.

If things get a little too hectic, you can press the Shift key to call in an air-strike and clear the screen. You can also grab bricks from the building and lob them at the ground, which will take out multiple elves with one shot.

The Kingdom of Loathing

Asymmetric Publications

First released in early 2003, *The Kingdom of Loathing* is a browser-based RPG that doesn't take itself too seriously. Your *KoL* journey is told through crudely drawn black-and-white environments and hilarious encounters with a variety of absurd characters.

While exploring the world, the hero encounters different enemies and monsters and must defeat them via turn-based combat. Quests are displayed on a panel to the left of the action, and players can level up by completing these challenges and by killing baddies. Every element of the game aims to be humorous, from the silly weapons to the random cocktail-crafting. *KoL* players are known for their use of proper grammar and spelling, and will correct anyone using Internet-speak like "lol."

The Kingdom of Loathing has proved so popular that creators Zack "Jick" Johnson and Josh "Mr. Skullhead" Nite are now able to employ a team of five to work on the game full-time, thanks to user donations and merchandise sales. The game was still considered unfinished at the time of writing, as new content is added frequently.

http://indiegam.es/playKoL

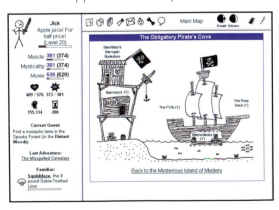

The Last Stand

Con Artist Games

How would you survive a zombie apocalypse? *The Last Stand* puts you in the role of a survivor who has barricaded himself behind a wall and must fend zombies off every night, whilst heading out in the day to look for supplies and survivors.

You start off with just a pistol. As you play, you'll need to allocate your time between searching for new weapons, repairing your barricade, and looking for other humans to help you survive. It's a trade-off; more powerful weapons will let you take the zombies down more quickly, but having more survivors on your team allows you to fortify your wall more quickly and provides extra firepower in battle.

The Last Stand has proved to be a huge success, with over 10 million plays in total. A sequel called *The Last Stand 2* has already been released, and another game in the series—*The Last Stand: Union City*—is currently in production.

http://indiegam.es/PlayLastStand

Line Rider

Boštjan Cadež

First released in 2006, *Line Rider* quickly became an Internet phenomenon thanks to its entertaining premise and sandbox-style tools. Players draw a series of lines, and then a boy on a sled rides along them until he either crashes or reaches the end of the run.

There is no real goal in *Line Rider*—instead, this is a game about letting your imagination run wild. The sled can pick up some serious speed depending on the angle of the slope you draw, and you can introduce elements like loop-the-loops, which will propel him to another place in the level. As long as his head doesn't hit the floor, the ceiling, or the walls, he'll keep racing along. More experienced users have used the tools to create some incredible runs, many of which are featured on the *Line Rider* website.

The success of the game has spawned multiple commercial versions, including a sequel for PC and the Nintendo Wii and Nintendo DS, along with an app for the iPhone and the iPad.

http://indiegam.es/playLineRider

Powder Game

DAN-BALL

Powder Game is a sandbox wind simulator that offers players a variety of different materials to blow around the screen. Players can experiment with different effects, and even add little stick men who will fight each other in the world you've created.

The available materials react differently to wind, fans, bubbles, and other forces, and playing around with everything that's on offer is rather addictive. Powder and salt particles will whirl around the screen, while nitro and blocks of C-4 cause psychedelic explosions. You can control some of your stick men via the arrow keys, and subject them to fire, acid, lasers, and bombs if you want. Birds and ants add a pleasantly natural atmosphere to your world.

Once you've created your world, you can upload it so that other players will be able to play and rate it. You can also play levels by other players, and there are numerous great creations to be found.

http://indiegam.es/playPowderGame

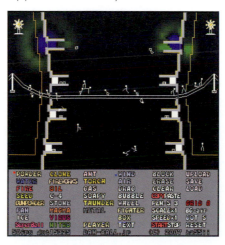

Dino Run

Pixeljam Games

If you ever wondered why dinosaurs became extinct, *Dino Run* has the answer. Your job is to get your dinosaur to safety by running as fast as possible from a huge wall of death that's sweeping the land.

There will be eggs to collect and smaller dinosaurs to gobble up (it's a dino-eat-dino world out there) as you flee from certain doom. Each level features a variety of secrets to uncover, hidden routes to explore, and awards to obtain—not to mention skins to dress your dinosaur in, and hats to adorn his bony head. You'll earn DNA and upgrade your dino's abilities if you get far enough. There are also multiple game modes at your disposal that feature speed runs and different challenges.

Once you've mastered the single-player courses, the multiplayer races will keep you entertained for even longer. There's a ranked levelling system in place so that you can find suitable opponents online.

http://indiegam.es/playDinoRun

Gravity Hook

Adam "Atomic" Saltsman and Danny Baranowsky

Gravity Hook takes place in a secret base underground. An unnamed hero wonders how far below the surface he is and uses his Gravity Hook to fling himself upward as far as he can so that he can find out.

The game can feel a little tricky to control at first, but once you get the hang of it, the action is great fun. Clicking on one of the floating mines will allow the protagonist to fire his hook and latch on to it so that he can spring into the air. However, latching on to a mine will cause it to open up, revealing the explosives inside—and if the hero touches the mine in this form, he will die. His speed is controlled by his proximity to the mines, and you'll find the gameplay to be rather fast-paced as you attempt to constantly shift from mine to mine and stay aloft.

The game was inspired by a typing-tutor prototype called *Gravity Key*, which was developed by Arne Niklas Jansson. An updated commercial version, *Gravity Hook HD*, is also available for the iPhone and iPad.

http://indiegam.es/playGH

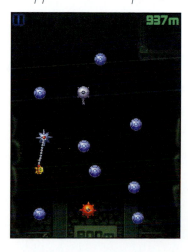

You Have to Burn the Rope

Mazapan

In early 2008, developer Mazapan decided to push the limits of what could be described as a game. *You Have to Burn the Rope* features the absolute minimal elements of gaming—that is, an objective and a result—and was created solely to make fun of the limited interaction in other games.

You Have to Burn the Rope lasts around a minute in total, and your goal is plain and simple—burn a rope to win. The game is a commentary on the point at which these kinds of simple and linear experiences cease to be games. After you've completed your task, an amusing song will play to further emphasize the game's ironic statement.

Despite its brevity, *You Have to Burn the Rope* has been played online more than 3.6 million times and has also been showcased at various game exhibitions. It was nominated for the Innovation award at the 2009 Independent Games Festival.

http://indiegam.es/playYHTBTR

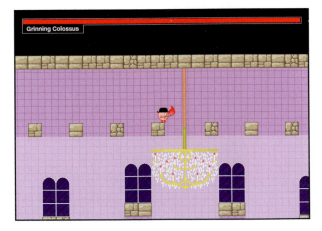

Captain Forever

Jarrad "Farbs" Woods

The *Captain Forever* series is a sandbox exploration game set in deep space. You are the captain of the Nemesis, stranded in the middle of nowhere with randomly-generated enemies all around.

Fortunately, you have a weak laser that's sufficient to pick off less powerful opponents. Once you've destroyed a ship, you can gather the remnants (that include things like body parts, thrusters, and lasers) and attach them to your ship with your mouse. Updates to your ship allow you to tackle more powerful enemies and steal their parts too. Eventually it's possible to build yourself a huge ship that is capable of taking down anything that comes within range.

You can play *Captain Forever* for free, or set up an account on the site to access a variety of advanced, pay-for-play versions of the game—such as *Captain Successor* and *Captain Impostor*—that add new modes and more ship pieces to play around with.

http://indiegam.es/playCP

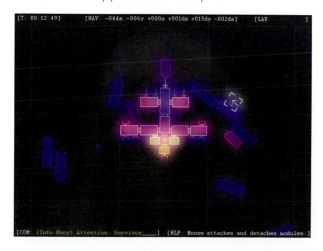

Little Wheel

OneClickDog

When a terrible accident at the main power generator occurs, an entire city of robots runs out of energy and the whole population switches off. Ten thousand years later, a freak bolt of lightning hits a tower where a small robot lies, waking him from his dormancy.

Little Wheel follows this robot's story as he attempts to reach the main generator and turn the power back on. The game is a point-and-click adventure, so in each area there are various items for him to interact with, and the robot forges a path by experimenting with these interactions. The game is short (taking roughly 15 minutes to complete) but entertaining, and worth playing for the gorgeous visuals and jazzy music alone.

Little Wheel received a huge amount of coverage in the mainstream press when it was released, and won the award for best browser game at the MTV Game Awards in 2009.

http://indiegam.es/playLittleWheel

Continuity

Ragtime Games

Continuity combines your standard sliding-tile puzzle with a simple platforming game, and the result is something rather wonderful. You play by shuffling the tiles in each level around into configurations that allow your stick-man hero to progress.

Your goal is to get the edges of two adjacent tiles to match, and once you've done that, your hero will be able to move between them and onto a new tile. Then you can shuffle the tiles again and move him into a brand new area. If you play your cards right, you'll be able to reach the key and help him escape through the red door.

The game has picked up multiple high-profile awards, including the Best Student Game at the 2010 Gameplay Independent Game Festival and the Gameplay Innovation Award at IndieCade 2010. A sequel is currently in the works for the iPhone and is expected to be released sometime in 2011.

http://indiegam.es/playContinuity

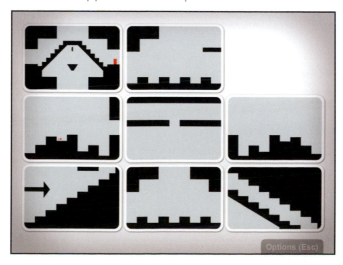

Use Boxmen

Greg Sergeant

Use Boxmen is a tricky platform puzzler whose premise is exactly what it says on the tin. The main character can create clones of himself to interact with the surroundings and help him safely obtain the special box that's located somewhere in the level.

The clones act in a variety of roles (from runners to blockers to crouchers) determined by how the protagonist is standing, so you may be reminded of the classic game *Lemmings*. *Use Boxmen* is a charming game, with the narrator noting that both he and the hero are aware that they are in a video game, and the clones displaying beaming smiles regardless of their fates.

The game caused quite a stir in the mainstream media, even winning the 2009 E4 Platform Game of the Year award. It has been played more than 30 million times to date.

http://indiegam.es/playboxmen

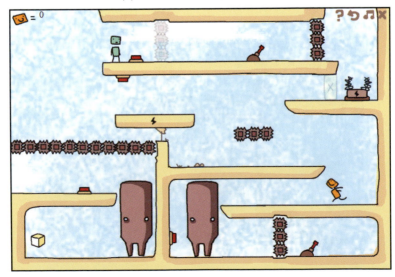

Exploit

Gregory Weir

It's time to stand up to totalitarianism and government abuses of power! *Exploit* is a grid-based puzzle game about hacking, in which you fire off packets of data so that you can break through firewalls to find the information you need.

Each system has a root node that you'll need to access, but there are digital obstacles all over the place designed to prevent security breaches (like blocker nodes that will stop your packets from reaching their destinations, and divider nodes that will cause them to change direction). An in-depth tutorial explains all the different node types. The action is relatively simple when it starts off, but eventually you'll find yourself up against some seriously complex systems.

Story mode features a great plot with solid writing in between each level, while challenge mode throws a selection of head-scratchers your way. You can even create your own security systems by using the puzzle editor that's included.

http://indiegam.es/playExploit

Time Fcuk

Edmund McMillen and William Good

Time Fcuk is a platforming game that takes pleasure in being nonsensical. The "you" from 20 minutes in the future appears and tells you to get into a box. You're then presented with a variety of tricky plane-switching puzzles.

Reaching the portal on each level is always the goal, but the portals are not always immediately accessible. The switch-plane button is your key to success, as it allows the hero to move between dimensions and create platforms that were not originally present. If the portal is on another plane, you may need to switch between planes multiple times to reach it, especially in the game's later levels. You can also create your own *Time Fcuk* levels, and there are tons of user-created puzzles to play in addition to the game's basic mode.

Time Fcuk was developed for the Newgrounds Power of Three festival, in which three game designers worked individually within a team to produce the art, code, and music for a game. The music and the haunting sounds in *Time Fcuk* were created by Justin Karpel.

http://indiegam.es/playTimeFcuk

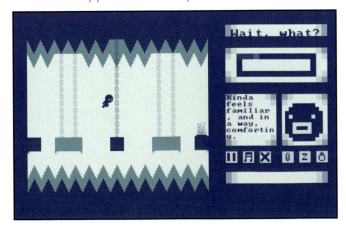

Small Worlds

David Shute

Small Worlds implements pixel art in a unique manner: it begins with a claustrophobic, blocky setting that slowly reveals itself to be far more detailed as you explore.

As you move around, the camera pans out to capture each of the areas you've explored, and piece by piece the scene will be built up into something beautiful. It's as if your protagonist, in the process of becoming more familiar with the surroundings, realizes that what originally appeared to be a bit of a mess is actually a highly detailed world. Each different area tells a story—through images rather than text—and piecing them all together is really fantastic stuff.

The game was developed for the sixth Casual Gameplay Design competition, for which the theme was "Explore." It not only won first prize, but also the Audience Award.

http://indiegam.es/playSmallWorlds

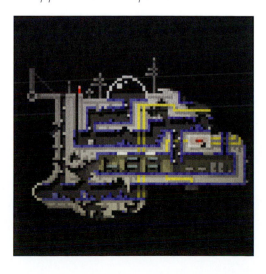

Blasting Agent

Tim "SeiferTim" Hely and Robert "Darthlupi" Lupinek

An international terrorist group calling itself "The Black Hand of Fate" has secretly built a huge weapons facility in the heart of a volcano in Antarctica. Only the Blasting Agent can stop its army of genetically-created monsters and bio-engineered soldiers.

The Blasting Agent is you, of course—a secret agent with a nice fat blaster. The hero ventures into the harsh environment, gunning down enemies with his laser and taking on huge boss battles. Throughout the mission, you'll find a multitude of weapon upgrades, treasures, and health pick-ups to collect that will help turn the tide of battle your way. If you play well enough, there are awards to bag, and a more difficult level is available if you manage to blast your way to victory in easy mode.

The game is rather short, with only three levels to play, but unlocking absolutely everything in the game will test the skills of even the best players.

http://indiegam.es/playBA

Evacuation

Ben Foddy and Ryan Chisholm

Evacuation is a puzzle game set in space that features decompression chambers, coloured gates, and hungry aliens that cause mayhem for your ship's crew. On each level, your goal is to eject the aliens into space without losing any of your people.

This is easier said than done; all the gates between chambers are colour-coded, and opening one gate will open all gates of the same colour. That means it's easy to accidentally remove crew members along with the aliens. Fortunately, you can command your crew to move into different rooms—but just make sure you don't lead them into an alien-infested area, as the big purple blobs are rather ravenous.

Note that while you can sacrifice part of your crew without ending the game, Captain Ryan—the officer in the control room at the front of the ship—must be kept alive at all costs.

http://indiegam.es/playEvacuation

The Company of Myself

Eli Piilonen and Luka Marcetic

A man who once had a lot of friends now spends his life alone and wonders where it all went wrong. Fortunately, he's capable of performing some pretty neat cloning tricks to help get himself past some of life's toughest obstacles.

The Company of Myself plays with the idea of interacting with past versions of yourself. The hero can move into position, then materialize again and watch his past self make the same move that he just did. This ability allows him to jump on the heads of his past selves to reach ledges that were originally too high for him to leap onto. Later on he'll have to act as a makeshift platform for his clones.

The protagonist explains his thoughts and how his past fits into the gameplay as the action unfolds. At the time of writing, the game had been played nearly five million times.

http://indiegam.es/playCOM

Tower of Heaven

Askiisoft

Tower of Heaven follows a mysterious protagonist as he attempts to climb a dangerous tower by moving through a sequence of increasingly difficult rooms. During his ascent, an unnamed adversary taunts him and will do anything to prevent him from reaching the top.

A special resource called the Book of Laws is introduced early in the game, and players must follow rules like "Thou shalt not touch golden blocks" and "Thou shalt not walk left" or see their lives end abruptly. The laws are added one by one over the course of the 11 levels. By the time you reach the last few rooms, all the laws will be in effect at the same time and the going will be very tough.

The game was originally developed in 2009 by Askiisoft as a freeware download. It was later released as a Flash browser title with help from indie developers Miroslav Malesevic and Stefan Jeremic.

http://indiegam.es/playTOH

You Only Live Once

Marcus "Raitendo" Richert

You Only Live Once is more like a conceptual cartoon than a playable game. Players find themselves in a Mario-like world with a twist: if you die, there is no way to play the game again, even if you reload your browser or refresh the page.

The game is simple but unforgiving, and your chances of completing it are very slim. Once the main character has died, you'll be treated to a series of game-over screens (a new one shows up each time the page is refreshed). The screens range from a television broadcast announcing your death to a shot of your grave with grass growing from the soil; refresh the page enough times and your character will begin to rise from the dead, only to fall over dead again.

This experimental game was presented by developer Marcus Richert at the 2009 Sense of Wonder Night in Tokyo. Keita Takahashi, developer of *Katamari Damacy*, said he liked the game's "corniness."

Today I Die

Daniel Benmergui

Today I Die follows a girl as she descends into the darkness. Words at the top of the screen describe the scene that's being displayed, but players can change the words to help the girl escape her dark fate.

As you drag new words into place the scene changes accordingly. However, not every word is available at the beginning so you'll need to interact with the scene itself to uncover more words. The correct combination of words will allow the girl to move away from the dark and eventually escape into the light. Later scenarios are more difficult to figure out and you'll probably have to experiment with the demons around the girl to work out how to help her progress.

An iPhone version of the game called *Today I Die Again* is also available; it follows the same format but features a different set of events and words.

http://indiegam.es/playTID

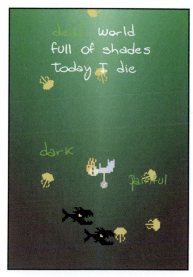

DefeatMe

Kenta Cho

In *DefeatMe*, your greatest enemy is yourself; at each stage, you fight clones of yourself who repeat your moves from previous rounds—including firing back at you.

Each level includes clones of all your past selves; therefore, by the time you reach double figures, the screen will be filled with laser fire and winning will be next to impossible. So what's the best tactic: firing off as few bullets as possible, or spraying and dodging all over the place? You won't have a chance to sit back and think about it, as a laser wall is constantly moving down the screen and you'll be killed instantly if it reaches the bottom.

DefeatMe is hosted on the Wonderfl coding site, where users can copy each other's code and create their own spinoffs—hence, there are also plenty of "forked" versions of *DefeatMe* to play.

http://indiegam.es/playDefeatMe

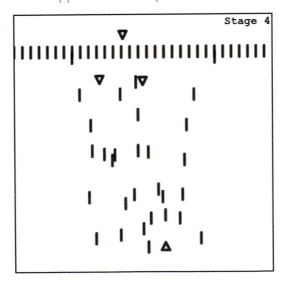

Closure

Tyler Glaiel and Jon Schubbe

Closure is a gloomy platformer that follows one simple rule: if an obstacle is shrouded in darkness, then it no longer exists. Only light can bring walls, ceilings, and floors into full view, and fortunately the game's protagonist has an abundance at his disposal.

The hero starts each level with a ball of light that he carries around to illuminate platforms. He'll soon come up against a wall or two, at which point he can use the darkness to his advantage by dropping the ball on the floor so that the upper part of the wall is no longer lit up. Now that the wall doesn't exist, he can jump through the darkness and past the obstacle. This is just one of many clever puzzles that *Closure* will throw at you, as the concept is explored to its fullest.

Spurred on by a win at the Independent Games Festival in 2010, not to mention more than one million online plays, the *Closure* team is currently working on a commercial version of the game.

http://indiegam.es/playClosure

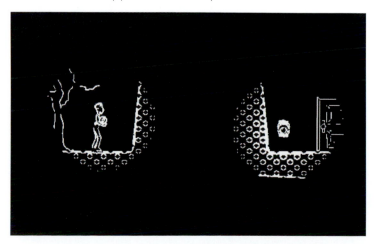

Canabalt

Semi Secret Software

Developer Adam Saltsman came up with the name of this game after he heard his nephew mispronounce the word "catapult." *Canabalt* is a platforming game with one-button play; players hit the space bar (or touch the screen in the iPhone version) to jump over obstacles and leap through gaps between buildings.

The protagonist dashes along rooftops and smashes through windows, although we never discover exactly what it is he is running away from. Levels are randomly generated, so no two playthroughs are ever the same. It is impossible to "win" *Canabalt* as our hero never reaches his destination—rather, the goal is to see how far you can run before falling. The game has been hugely popular due to its simple yet addictive gameplay and the gorgeous futuristic sci-fi setting. The mysterious nature of its story has further enhanced its appeal.

Canabalt has inspired a whole new genre of Flash and iPhone games, including the Spiritonin Media title *Robot Unicorn Attack*.

http://indiegam.es/playcanabalt

Icycle

Reece "Damp Gnat" Millidge

When you're waking up from a cryogenically frozen state, the last thing you'd expect to see is a bicycle in the pod next to yours. Nevertheless, this is what happens in *Icycle*, and the naked hero is all too happy to jump on the bike and pedal his way through treacherously cold landscapes.

Someone else has been unthawed at the same time, and your task is to chase your unnamed quarry down. The protagonist can cycle forwards but not backwards, so you'll have to anticipate the moves you'll need to make in order to solve each of the puzzles that presents itself. As you progress through the game's eight levels, backdrops tell the story of what has happened on Earth while you were frozen.

There are also frozen bubbles throughout each level to collect—developer Reece Millidge says that this idea was inspired by a gorgeous collection of frozen soap bubble images that he spotted online.

http://indiegam.es/playIcycle

Mountain Maniac

Pixeljam Games

The Mountain Man is in a bit of a rage, and he's venting his anger on the city below. In *Mountain Maniac,* you slam the mountaintop with your hammer, creating huge boulders that roll down and destroy anything in their paths.

As the boulders fall, you hit the left and right arrows to guide them into as many cars, trees, animals, and houses as possible—and you'll rack up huge combos if you manage to take out multiples of the same obstacles. Eventually, the boulder reaches the bottom of the mountain, and you'll need to lay waste to a certain proportion of the city's buildings to progress. At the end of each level, law enforcers will appear at the top of the mountain to arrest you, but fortunately you've got your trusty hammer to hold them back.

Mountain Maniac was developed as part of a series of 8-bit games that were created during a collaboration between Adult Swim Games and Pixeljam Games. Other games in the series include *Sausage Factory*, *Turbo Granny*, and *Creamwolf*.

http://indiegam.es/playMM

When the Bomb Goes Off

Tom Sennett

What will you be doing when the world ends? This is the question asked by *When the Bomb Goes Off*, a humorous take on those last precious moments before total destruction. Your task is to help a variety of people achieve their goals before the bomb hits.

You're thrown into different situations one at a time and given five seconds to complete each task. Activities include catching an American football, swinging from a chandelier, and passing a drink to a friend at a party. It's hard to tell whether you've completed the assignments until the end of the game, when you'll get a display that shows the percentage of tasks that were completed.

The game features a few nods to classic video games; in one scenario, you jump over a Mario-style pipe and land on an opponent similar to a Koopa Troopa. Tom has also remarked that Nintendo's *WarioWare* series had a big influence on the game's design.

http://indiegam.es/play WTBGO

Time4Cat

Megadev

A stray cat stumbles upon a special collar that allows the wearer to control time. The feline sets out during a busy lunch break and uses the collar's unique power to collect the morsels of food dropped by busy, clumsy workers.

You control the cat's movements with your mouse. The time-altering mechanics of the game are rather clever—the people around the cat only move when he does, so if the cat is stationary, everyone surrounding him will be too. However, each piece of food has a time limit on it and must be collected before the timer hits zero; hence, the cat cannot stand around for too long. The volume of pedestrian traffic will rise along with your score, making it more difficult for the cat to reach the leftovers. If a human steps on you, the game is over.

Mysterious glowing white balls will appear occasionally, and collecting these will allow the cat to push people away from him, thereby reducing the risk of being trampled.

http://indiegam.es/playTime4Cat

Don't Look Back

Terry Cavanagh

A take on the story of Orpheus and Eurydice from Greek mythology, *Don't Look Back* is a short but powerful platformer that follows Orpheus as he journeys into the Underworld on a quest to find his love. The game features a simple, yet striking, graphical style and tough platforming action. There are also boss fights against the deities of the Underworld.

The majority of the areas in *Don't Look Back* can be navigated by observing the movement patterns of your enemies and dodging them accordingly. Once you've managed to find Eurydice, you'll need to bring her back to the surface—although, if you are familiar with the original story, you know that this will be rather tricky!

Many gamers have commented on how impressive it is that the lo-fi visuals can give such a creepy feel. The game has received roughly one million plays since its release in early 2009, helping launch developer Terry Cavanagh into the limelight.

http://indiegam.es/playDLB

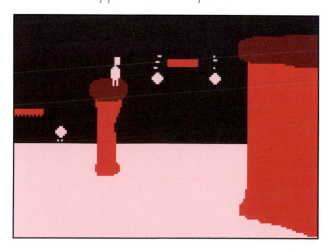

Chase Goose 2

Andres "Hideous" Jörgensen and Jacob "Sereneworx" Zinman-Jeanes

There's a snake monster on the loose that's rather fond of eating geese. You are one such goose, trying to escape as the monster edges closer and closer by tapping furiously away on your keyboard.

Escape might be simple were it not for the deliberately awkward control scheme. To make our feathered friend run, you'll need to keep alternating the left and right arrows—but that's not all. Whenever there is a gap in the floor, you'll need to tap whatever keyboard button is displayed on the screen (and it can be anything), so a good knowledge of your keyboard is a must! Eventually the key play gets even trickier, as you're required to hold down the Shift key the entire time, and will need to know such random trivia as the "Japanese Lucky Number."

This sequel builds on the original game by adding more polish and by requiring players to use many more keys. Both games will give your arm a thorough workout, though, as the constant tapping will really get your muscles going.

http://indiegam.es/playChaseGoose

(I Fell in Love With) The Majesty of Colors

Gregory Weir

The Majesty of Colors is one person's dream about being a huge squid-like creature from the deep. A single playthrough lasts just a few minutes, during which you control the squid's long tentacle and choose whether to interact with the human race in a positive or negative manner.

The title of the game refers to the first time the sea creature plucks a colourful balloon from the sky and examines it with his huge eyeballs. Players can choose to help out the humans—for example, by catching fish for a fisherman or by saving a child from a shark attack—or they can decide to drown anyone who goes into the water and then deal with the subsequent human retaliation.

There are five endings in total, and story paths go in different directions depending on how you deal with each situation. *The Majesty of Colors* is widely regarded as one of Gregory's finest pieces of work.

http://indiegam.es/playMajesty

Feign

Ian Snyder

Feign puts your ideas of perspective to the test as you attempt to navigate a twisted maze that at times does not appear to be passable. Along the way, you must find and save nine glowing people.

From the very beginning, *Feign*'s level design doesn't appear to make any sense, as corridors seem to open out into areas that appeared at first to be empty space. Players must think outside of the box to succeed in *Feign*, as there is a multitude of mind-bending twists and turns to overcome. One way to prevail is to stick to the walls of the maze whenever you find yourself lost—you may find that an opening presents itself in a place where it seemed impossible to encounter an outlet.

Finding the final person is tricky, so here's a hint: try ignoring the rules of the game, and you may find that the ninth character will appear when you reach the end.

http://indiegam.es/playFeign

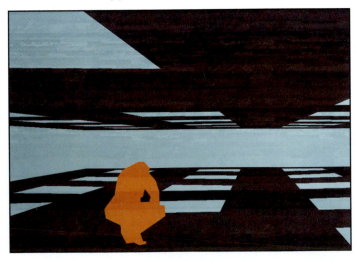

GROW Cube

Eyezmaze

Browser game *GROW Cube* revolves around the idea of building up a small world on the surface of a cube. You're given ten different objects, and the animations you see will depend on the order in which you apply them.

As you add more items to the cube, every object on the cube will react in either a positive or negative manner and will evolve to fit the scene. Once all ten objects have been placed, a level that shows the degree to which each has evolved will be displayed next to each element. The idea is to find the perfect ordering of the objects, so that each can reach MAX evolution and you can play the final animation.

GROW Cube is the third in the *GROW* series, which is currently comprised of more than a dozen games—including a Christmas tree edition and an RPG—with a similar concept. Many of the *GROW* games have secret endings in addition to the basic ones, and you'll usually have to think "outside the box" to find them.

http://indiegam.es/playGROWcube

One Button Bob

Tom "Ninjadoodle" Vencel

Help One Button Bob traverse a dangerous castle and find a treasure via the simple click of a mouse button. You click anywhere in the game to make Bob perform various actions—like jumping over pits or running away from heavy boulders Indiana Jones style.

Controlling Bob is different on each screen and will depend on the obstacle he's facing. When there are bats and spiders, he'll throw his trusty boomerang to cut them down; if an arrow trap is the problem, holding the mouse button will make Bob pause for a moment so that he can avoid it. A tally of the number of times you've clicked is displayed in the top corner so that you can compare how well you did with friends.

A sequel to *One Button Bob* is also available: *One Button Arthur* features the same style of one-button gaming but with play that's more focussed on navigating small rooms than on walking in a straight line.

http://indiegam.es/playOBB

You Have No Legs

Martin Brochu

You Have No Legs follows the story of Jack, an archaeologist who is working at a dig site in Teotihuacan, Mexico, when a huge earthquake rocks the land and a fissure swallows him up. He is trying to escape from his tomb, but there's one problem—he has no legs.

The game features a rather interesting method for getting Jack around: you click and hold the mouse button in front of Jack to make him grab the floor, and then drag backward, which allows him to pull himself along. After exploring the cavern, you'll find power-ups that let Jack climb walls and hurl himself through the air to safety. Small pools of water are scattered around that act as save points in your journey.

The game was developed for the fifth Game Developer Challenge at SomethingAwful.com, where it won first place.

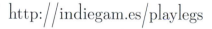

http://indiegam.es/playlegs

Solipskier

Mikengreg (Mike Boxleiter and Greg Wohlwend)

Solipskier is a fast-paced arcade game about skiing at alarming speeds. You hold down your mouse button to draw a slalom for your skier, and then guide him through gates and tunnels to build up his velocity.

Along the way, there are red gates that must be dodged and areas where you can't draw any snow courses. Therefore, it is essential to plan ahead and flick the skier into the air whenever one of these sections is approaching, which will enable him to perform stunts above the troublesome parts. If the skier reaches breakneck speeds, his headphones will fly off, and the rock music will be replaced with the sound of wind as it rushes past his ears.

Within a month of release, the game had been played roughly four million times. The game is also available on both the iPhone and Android.

Hummingbird Mind

Jake Elliott

Hummingbird Mind is a short adventure game with a rather unique premise: it follows the thoughts of a man who suffers from attention deficit disorder and who is constantly being distracted from his work by things in his apartment.

In the beginning, you won't be able to choose all the actions and line of dialogue that are available; some will be blacked out until you've gathered information and have been able to make some progress in the game. The protagonist creates whole conversations in his head, playing out the types of arguments his cat would make if the cat could talk, and the dialogue is witty and rather poetic in places.

The main reason to play *Hummingbird Mind*, though, is the great feeling it will leave behind after you've finished. Developer Jake Elliott has said that he is interested in creating non-violent games with themes such as friendship, collaboration, and community, and he's definitely succeeded with this release.

http://indiegam.es/playhummingbird

Achievement Unlocked

John Cooney

If you're obsessed with collecting gamerscore on your Xbox 360 or trophies on your Playstation 3, *Achievement Unlocked* may well speak straight to your heart. John Cooney developed the game as a satirical look at the popularity of achievement harvesting.

You take control of a small blue elephant and your goal is to unlock every single achievement from a huge list. However, the achievements aren't exactly difficult to unlock—in fact, one is awarded for simply loading up the game, while another is given for moving the elephant to the right. The achievements are purposely silly and simple to unlock, and each achievement also has a hint that makes it more than obvious how to accomplish it. "Winning" is based on the sheer quantity of achievements you accumulate, rather than how challenging the achievements themselves are.

The game is hugely popular, with over four million plays to date. The now-famous blue elephant has since appeared in many of John's releases, including the tricky *This Is the Only Level* and the inevitable *Achievement Unlocked 2*.

http://indiegam.es/playAchievement

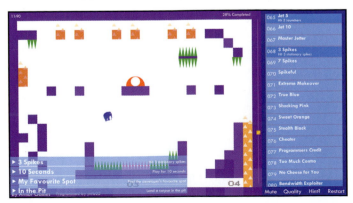

[Together]

Michael "Bean" Molinari

[Together] follows the story of a young man and woman who take off into the sky, fleeing from an unknown dark monster as they try to collect hearts. There is no real explanation for the couple's voyage, although the underlying metaphors are quite clear.

The lovers are guided by your mouse pointer, and can zip around the sky or dive into the ocean to look for hearts in the depths. When they catch up with a heart you'll need to keep the mouse pointer steady so that they can grab it, then click to give them a short speed boost that will let them race away from the monster. The monster can also be pushed back by performing small circular movements with the mouse. Each element of the game is a metaphor for love—especially the ending, if you manage to find it.

The game was developed for the eighth Casual Gameplay Design competition, for which it took the third place prize.

http://indiegam.es/playTogether

One Step Back

Daniel Yaroslavski

Forgetting troublesome times from your past can be difficult, especially if you live in the world of *One Step Back*. The hero must reach the exit on each level, but cannot bump into past versions of himself as he makes his way there.

This is a little difficult, as clones of his past come forth from the entrance door every few steps and mimic his movements exactly. At the beginning of the game the exit door is not always available, and in the meantime the protagonist must weave around his ghosts making sure not to touch them. Note that his past selves will not move unless he is moving, so it's possible to stop and plan a route before implementing it.

One Step Back was inspired by a variety of well-known indie titles, especially those that play around with the concept of time-bending and cloning yourself—these include the likes of *Braid* and *Company of Myself*.

http://indiegam.es/playOSB

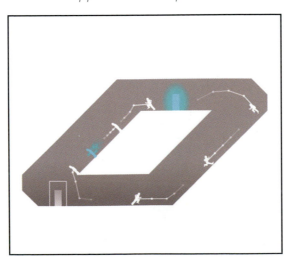

Every Day
the Same Dream

Molleindustria

In *Every Day the Same Dream,* you are tasked with helping a faceless worker break free from his monotonous life and take steps towards finding a new path. The game is presented in a mostly monochromatic style, with a rather depressing soundtrack to match the mood.

Players can choose to simply get dressed, head out to work, sit in the cubicle, and get shouted at by the boss—but there are many opportunities to break from the norm, whether it's skipping certain elements of the day or just trying to find a way around the normal routine. A wise lady in the elevator keeps track of your attempts to break away as you play the same sequence over and over.

The game was developed in just six days for the Experimental Gameplay "Art Game" theme, and it received tremendous praise online. A short film based on the game's storyline was even created, which was directed by Patryk Senwicki and Tamas Kiss.

http://indiegam.es/playEDTSD

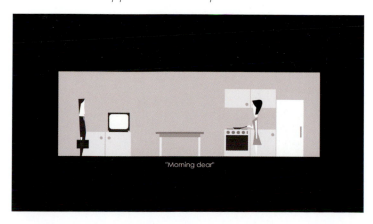

Samorost

Amanita Design

Samorost is a surreal point-and-click adventure game that features a gorgeous visual style and a very simple approach to exploring. Players control a hero who has spotted a spiky meteor heading straight for his planet, and therefore sets off in a rocket to alter its course.

In each different area, players scour the screen looking for items to click on, and your white-clothed fellow will only progress if you deal with these interactions in the correct order. The story is told through visuals with barely any text, making *Samorost* a unique but worthwhile experience. Amanita Design is now best known for its unique graphical style, and the high standards applied to *Samorost* have been carried forward into other releases.

The sequel, simply called *Samorost 2*, is also available to play online. Only the first part of the sequel is free; the second half will cost you five dollars to download.

http://indiegam.es/playSamorost

Faultline

Nitrome

Faultline features a clever puzzling mechanic that makes for some unique platforming action. The main character is a robot who can launch his hands out to grab hold of nodes in the level. These nodes can then be folded over each other, hiding entire sections of the level from view.

With areas of the level now "in the void," you can pass freely through sections that were originally solid. For example, if there is a wall blocking your path, you can simply pull two nodes together on either side of the wall and it will disappear between them. Anything can be removed from play with this method—from ceilings to traps to enemies! Later levels provide more of a challenge, as there will be multiple nodes and you'll need to work out which ones are the best to utilise.

Nitrome is a London-based development team that's well known for its clever, unique gameplay mechanics, not to mention its chiptune music and lovely pixel art.

http://indiegam.es/playFaultline

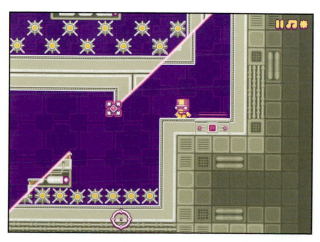

The Linear RPG

Sophie Houlden

The Linear RPG distils the role-playing game genre down to its simplest form. Players run along a series of straight lines, gaining experience from "battles" and visiting "inns" to replenish their health.

Enemy fights are automated, as are the damage and experience you receive. As you move along the black lines, stars will spring into the air if you've received damage, and if your health drops to zero, you'll rematerialize at the last black dot. Each dot is an inn where players can replenish their health. During play, a story scrolls behind the action, and as you progress farther along the lines, the story goes with you.

The game was developed in under 48 hours for an RPG game jam on the RPGDX forums with the theme "LoFi." Developer Sophie Houlden notes that while her intention was simply to create a "bare minimum" RPG, many players believed that the game was meant as a criticism of the grinding nature of many modern releases.

http://indiegam.es/playLinearRPG

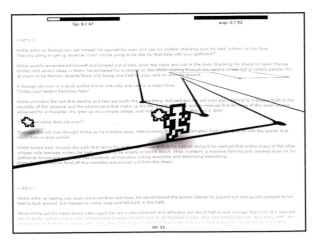

p0nd

The Peanut Gallery

On April 16, 2010, the famous American film critic and screenwriter Roger Ebert posted an entry to his online Chicago Sun-Times journal entitled "Video games can never be art." Ebert was inundated with comments from gamers who criticized his opinion, but developers at The Peanut Gallery chose to comment through the medium of game instead by releasing the rather twisted *p0nd*.

Players control a man who's on a brisk stroll through the woods; they hold the space bar so he can breathe in the fresh air and then release it to let him breathe out. Eventually, the man reaches a beautiful clearing with a lake, and a rather strange and completely unexpected scene occurs that throws the previously relaxing premise into total chaos.

The random and very silly series of events that follows aims to poke fun at Ebert's views, even quoting his words from a follow-up blog post in which he states "I may be wrong . . . ." There are multiple endings to find, depending on whether players manage to help the man breathe in time.

http://indiegam.es/playPond

Looming

Gregory Weir

Described by many players as a journey similar to the classic *Myst* (although perhaps not in visual style!), *Looming* follows an unnamed protagonist as he explores the plains of a mysterious world, finds clues, and uncovers a variety of beautiful intertwining stories.

You can tackle the mysteries of the monochromatic environment in any order you choose, and this exploration adventure will never make you feel rushed. *Looming* offers players a variety of events to experience, and the chance to accumulate an assortment of collectables throughout the game; as each set of items is gathered together, stories will reveal themselves, including one about two lovers and another about a band of people who don't believe that the sky exists.

There are nine endings, and the title screen will keep a record as you uncover each one so that you can reenter the world of *Looming* with your progress saved.

http://indiegam.es/playLooming

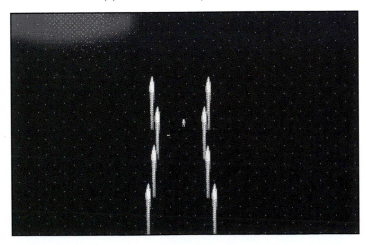

Action Turnip

Marcus "Raintendo" Richert

Only an indie game would give you the chance to take control of a turbo-charged turnip. This particular turnip is on the run, and the game has him dashing along platforms, entering psychedelic realms, and fighting off strange creatures with his laser fire.

As the turnip runs (leaving colourful rainbows in his wake), you can use your mouse to take aim and fire at an assortment of odd adversaries, but you'll need to use your keyboard at the same time to make sure that he doesn't fall through any gaps. If you rack up a nice combo (or die horribly), the ground will mould itself into words that you can run along. The amateur-looking graphical style changes over time and will cycle through a variety of scenes whose purpose is to confuse you and end the turnip's life.

This is not the first time the turnip has appeared in one of Marcus's games—it was also the protagonist in the equally strange *Free Will*.

http://indiegam.es/playActionTurnip

Crush the Castle

Joey Betz and Chris "Con" Condon

With over 20 million plays online, *Crush the Castle* has helped to make developers Joey Betz and Chris Condon famous. Players launch huge boulders at a series of castles with the goal of knocking down the structures and crushing the enemies inside.

Each stone is launched with two simple clicks: the first to get the trebuchet swinging and the second to let the rock fly. The action is entirely physics-based, meaning that if you strike the top of a castle, the upper pieces will collapse and possibly knock the remaining walls down too. Players need to crush every person in the castle to progress past a level, but there are only a limited number of rocks available for each scenario.

The game has enjoyed huge success, and both a sequel and an iPhone version have been released. It has also inspired a whole host of item-flinging games, including the hugely popular *Angry Birds* franchise.

http://indiegam.es/playCastle

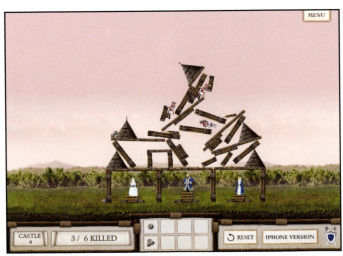

Entanglement

Gopherwood Studios

Entanglement is a clever tile-placing puzzler in which you position hexagons on a board in order to extend a spaghetti-like line for as long as possible, without letting it hit the sides of the hexagons that haven't been played.

Each hexagon has two lines extending from each edge, for a total of 12 different connection points. You place hexagons and rotate them, attempting to match a line from your hexagon with the red line that connects to the hexagon in the centre so that the centre red line is extended. The red line will zigzag around the board, going under and over itself as players add to its length. The more pieces the red line goes through before reaching a gap, the more points you will receive. Once the red line cannot move anywhere other than into a wall, your final score is recorded.

While the game will work with any web browser, it is best played in Google Chrome since it's a Chrome webstore app. Using a Google account will also allow you to upload your scores to an online leaderboard.

http://indiegam.es/playEntangle

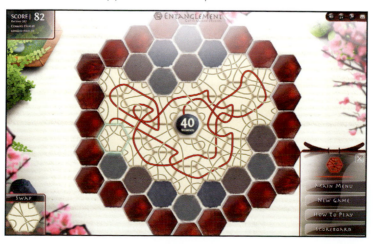

Run Jesus Run

Molleindustria

Run Jesus Run (aka *The 10 Second Gospel*) is a quick-fire and very silly look at the life of Jesus Christ. With ten seconds on the clock, you move hastily from his birth in Bethlehem to his crucifixion, performing miracles along the way.

The controls are as simple as the gameplay is; holding the right arrow causes Jesus to run, while pressing the space bar will make him "do Jesus things." Each screen covers a different story from the Gospel, including his trials in the desert with the devil, and his miracle of walking on water. At the end of the ten seconds—if you've managed to make it all the way without dying early—you'll be awarded a certain number of apostles out of a total of 12. The number you're awarded is based on the number of miracles that you successfully performed.

If you're wondering why the game is so short, it was developed in four days for an Experimental Gameplay Project competition with the theme "10 seconds."

http://indiegam.es/playJesus

Minotaur China Shop

Flashbang Studios

Minotaur China Shop takes the expression "bull in a china shop" and applies it to a game by putting you in control of the mythical Minotaur as he attempts to sell china plates and Ming vases to demanding customers.

As you'd expect, the Minotaur is rather difficult to control and not very well-suited to this kind of business—when he tries to retrieve a customer's selections from a shelf, there's every chance that the entire shelf will come crashing down instead. Fortunately, the Minotaur can benefit from his aggressive and destructive ways by ignoring his clientele and instead going on a rampage around the shop, which will result in a nice insurance payout. You'll be able to earn upgrades at the end of each day so that you can buy more stock for the shop and allow the beast to rage for a little longer.

Minotaur China Shop was one of Flashbang's first games to appear on its popular Blurst gaming site; it now plays host to many of the studio's classics, including *Blush* and *Time Donkey*.

http://indiegam.es/playMCS

Enough Plumbers

Glen Forrester and Arthur "Mr. Podunkian" Lee

Enough Plumbers features a Mario-like protagonist and a whole lot of clones. Every time the plumber grabs a coin, he'll generate a clone of himself, which highlights the clever puzzle-based level design and leads to some rather confusing platforming action.

The first several levels allow players time to figure out the cloning concept, and also introduce some special objects that can make the plumber heavy, fire-resistant, or weightless (much like in the Mario games). Eventually, you'll have to be more strategic about when and where you create your clones, or you may not reach the end. Fortunately, only one Mario has to reach the goal and it doesn't matter how many clones die in the process.

Enough Plumbers builds on a concept in a game previously released by developer Glen Forrester called *Enough Marios*. That game was created in under two hours for a Klik of the Month Klub jam, in which participants got together to create the silliest games they could think of on the spot.

http://indiegam.es/playPlumbers

PlayPen

Jarrad "Farbs" Woods

PlayPen is an online storybook told entirely by the players themselves through pixelated images. At each location you can either venture forward by selecting clickable areas, or edit the current screen to your heart's delight.

Players can edit the images displayed and add their own links to new areas by simply clicking "Draw here" (located at the bottom of any scene). They can then choose to create more content in new areas or leave them for other players to find and develop. In this way, thousands of players have created a rambling and somewhat twisted world full of oddities that can be explored and edited.

It's worth noting that the game is built on top of a software package known as MediaWiki, meaning that scenes are automatically recorded and can easily be restored if they're destroyed. It's not difficult to see why comparisons have been made between the way *PlayPen* and the web-based encyclopedia project Wikipedia work.

http://indiegam.es/PlayPlaypen

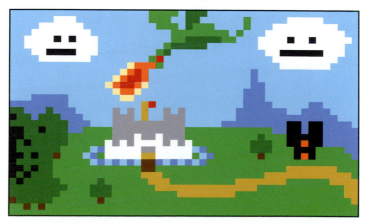

Poto & Cabenga

Honeyslug

Poto & Cabenga makes players adapt to a rather unique control scheme: manipulating two different characters with a single key. The game features a colourful alien rider who has been pulled from his faithful steed by a nasty flying creature, and the rider must run through the creature's belly to escape before it begins digesting.

You control both the rider at the top of the screen and the mount on the bottom by pressing and holding the space bar. Holding the space bar down causes the rider to jump into the air and the horse to dash forwards, and letting go makes the horse jump while the rider dashes forward. As adversaries approach, you'll need to help both characters leap out of harm's way so they can reach the end intact.

It's initially quite complicated and confusing, but eventually you'll find a rhythm and everything will fall into place. The game won a one-button competition called Gamma IV in 2010, and it was presented on the showroom floor at the Game Developers Conference in San Francisco the same year.

http://indiegam.es/playPoto

Quietus

Connor "Time" Ullmann

As he's taking a man's life, Death decides to have a little fun. He tells the man that he will give him his life back along with everything he ever wanted—if the man can survive the Gauntlet of Hell.

As you'd expect, the Gauntlet of Hell is not exactly the safest place to be. *Quietus* is a tricky platformer that requires quick reactions and lots of patience. Along the way, enemies and other obstacles impede your progress constantly by popping out of walls and moving into your path at the most inopportune moments. You will die a thousand deaths, but fortunately each annihilation brings with it only the modest penalty of taking you back to the beginning of the current room.

Along the way there are treasure chests—some in rather dangerous places—and players who manage to open every single one before reaching the end will be rewarded with a special ending.

http://indiegam.es/playQuietus

I Can Hold My Breath Forever

Jake Elliott

I Can Hold My Breath Forever follows a strange creature as it dives underwater in search of its friend. The creature cannot stay underwater for more than ten seconds, and in order to breathe, it must find caverns before the time runs out.

The friend has left notes in each cavern that tell the story of the creature as well as the story of the friendship. The creature is surrounded by darkness, and the moody soundtrack gives the experience a really powerful vibe. The ten-second time limit adds a sense of urgency but doesn't feel unfair—if you run out of air, you just get sent back to the last cavern you entered.

The game was developed for an Experimental Gameplay competition with the theme "10 Seconds," hence the underwater time limit.

http://indiegam.es/playBreath

Specter Spelunker Shrinks

Ken Grafals

The hero in *Specter Spelunker Shrinks* can grow and shrink rapidly, allowing him to climb up huge ledges or squeeze through tiny gaps. Over one short level, your task is to use this resizing ability to escape from a maze-like prison.

You need to push the protagonist's abilities to the limit, sometimes even expanding or shrinking in mid-air as you jump towards a gap. What makes *Specter Spelunker Shrinks* so wonderful is your changing sense of perspective as you play—one moment you'll be navigating a tiny maze, and the next you'll be growing to a huge size and using the entire previous area as a single platform.

Specter Spelunker Shrinks is currently the most played browser game on the indie gaming portal GameJolt, with more than 120,000 plays in total. Due to receiving a hugely positive response from the press, developer Ken Grafals is considering building on the concept at some point in the future.

http://indiegam.es/playSpecter

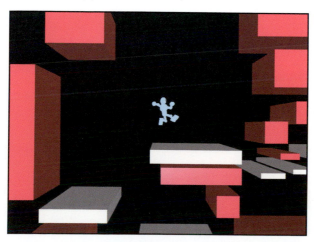

Redder

Anna "dessgeega" Anthropy

An astronaut is forced to make an emergency landing on a strange planet after her spaceship runs out of the crystals it uses for fuel. In *Redder*, you must dodge enemies as you explore underground ruins to find the crystals that will get your ship back into space.

The astronaut does not have a weapon, and instead must safely navigate around robots and laser fire. Along the way, you'll find switches to flick and clever puzzles to solve, and fortunately there are plenty of checkpoints so you can explore without worrying too much about getting killed. A world map is also available that can be used to travel to locations you have already visited.

Most of Anna's previous releases have been linear, with the disadvantage of—in Anna's words—"tying the player to a train track." *Redder* explores the idea of design "off the train tracks" and has a very *Metroid* feel to it.

http://indiegam.es/playRedder

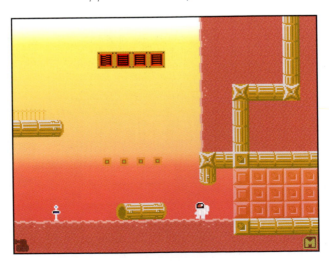

Record Tripping

Bell Brothers

Record Tripping is a unique and stylish offering from Bell Brothers in which you use your mouse wheel to emulate the back-and-forth "scratching" motion on a record. You're given a variety of tasks to complete while a record narrates Lewis Carroll's *Alice's Adventures in Wonderland* in the background, and the record will scratch and slow down with each move of your wheel.

There are easy, medium, and hard settings for each of the minigames and all five chapters are brimming with novel ideas. At one point, you'll be reading arrival times at a train station, then manipulating a clock so that you can bring a train into the station and the rabbits can hop on board. At another, you're asked to sort toys into the correct boxes as cats watch nearby nodding their heads to the beat of the music.

Many indie gamers have noted the exceptional use of music in this game, which includes featured tracks from bands such as Gorillaz and Spoon. *Record Tripping* won the Games award at the 14th annual Webby Awards.

http://indiegam.es/playRT

Depict1

Kyle Pulver

Developed in two days for the Global Game Jam 2010, *Depict1* features a shady character who is constantly trying to get you killed. Your goal in each room is simply to reach the exit—but when the game doesn't even tell you what the real controls are, this is easier said than done.

From the very beginning of the game, the dark figure feeds you incorrect information, and you're left to work out everything on your own (you may well find that there is more to be done even when it appears that the game has ended). Now and again the untrustworthy character will attempt to win back your confidence, but his intentions are never good.

Depict1 does a great job of making you question everything you've ever learned about platforming games, since so much of the gameplay is counterintuitive. Renowned indie developer and musician Alec Holowka provided the soundtrack for the game.

http://indiegam.es/playdepict1

Tumbledrop

Hayden "Dock" Scott-Baron

Far too cute for its own good, *Tumbledrop* is a physics-based balancing act that involves landing a smiling star on a platform surrounded by water. The star is perched precariously on top of a pile of blocks (each of which has its own beaming face), and you remove the blocks one by one in order to move the star onto the platform below.

The idea is to keep the pile balanced at all times so that the star will stay at the centre of the platform and away from the water. You cannot simply remove all the blocks rapidly, however, as there's a waiting period after you click each block before you can interact with the scene again. If the star begins to slip towards the sea, his face will show a look of terror before he disappears.

Thanks to its simple premise and colourful palette, *Tumbledrop* has proved very popular online, and many clones have appeared since the game's release. There is an iPhone version of *Tumbledrop* available too.

http://indiegam.es/playTumbledrop

Coma

Thomas Brush

Coma introduces Pete, a strange little man in an even stranger world that features gorgeous scenes and an assortment of surreal characters.

Pete can only run and jump, but he has a friendly bird that can pick up items for him. Pete's sister is mentioned quite often, although you're never explicitly told why. The idea is that this odd world that Pete is travelling through isn't actually real at all, and in fact Pete is simply dreaming while in a deep coma. Part of the game is discovering what each of the elements in the world symbolize—for example, it's safe to say that the "Dorebell" is a metaphor for Pete waking from his long sleep.

Coma deals with a number of creepy themes, and at times can be rather dark in its execution. The misspellings of certain words, along with the childlike acquaintances and environments, suggest that Pete is in fact a young boy.

http://indiegam.es/playComa

QWOP

Ben "Benzido" Foddy

Qwop is a small nation's only representative at the Olympic Games. Unfortunately, he wasn't given much training, and the simple act of running is so challenging for him that he constantly topples over during the 100-metre sprint.

You use the Q and W keys to pump the runner's thighs, and the O and P keys to move his calves. His body moves like a ragdoll, and it's incredibly difficult to run even a couple of metres—let alone the whole hundred! Players must work out the correct combination of button presses that will move Qwop forward, and then find a rhythm so that he'll pick up some speed. The game tracks your current best run, and a help screen gives a few hints as to how you can succeed and make your nation proud.

An iPhone version of *QWOP* is also available, which expands on the original browser version by adding other events like the hurdles, the long jump, and the 50-kilometre walk.

http://indiegam.es/playQwop

Endeavor

Alex "Zillix" Erlandson

A small dwarf's father discloses on his deathbed that a secret treasure chest, which has been passed down through the family, can be found somewhere in the world. The tiny hero sets out to claim the treasure for his own, and soon discovers more than he bargained for.

Initially, the protagonist is shunned by the other dwarves, who mock his size and ability. After falling from a great height, he is led by a being known as MALOP who asks the dwarf to collect a series of gems that will restore MALOP's power. Players collect flowers and plants throughout the game to upgrade the hero's abilities and allow him to venture farther into the world, and there is a plethora of quests and collectables to find. *Endeavor* also provides multiple endings, and the one you get will depend on how you play.

The game was originally created as a 48-hour Ludum Dare contest entry; after developer "Zillix" missed the deadline, he decided to continue development and expand the game's scope. The final product was released two months later.

http://indiegam.es/playEndeavor

Blue Knight

Ali Maunder

The Blue Knight has been sent to the planet ERA-138 to destroy the species of aliens there and make the planet suitable for colonisation. Players will find that power-ups are the key to helping the hero explore the land, since they'll enable him to venture into areas that he previously could not reach.

You'll need to dodge the various enemies at first, since you won't have a weapon at the beginning of the game, but early on you'll find a gun lying around and then the tables will turn. In fact, it's essential to kill everything you come across, as your opponents will drop crystals that you'll need to open special portals. *Blue Knight* is very much inspired by the *Metroid* series, in that adding power-ups such as your blaster or the diving suit is essential to allowing the protagonist to progress.

Once you've managed to kill all the gatekeepers, you'll be able to take on the boss alien and render planet ERA-138's current population extinct.

http://indiegam.es/playBlueKnight

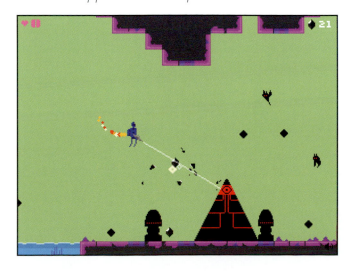

Mamono Sweeper

Hojamaka Games

Mamono Sweeper is a cross between the classic Windows game *Minesweeper* and an RPG. Instead of looking for mines, you hunt down monsters, and leveling up through experience allows you to kill even tougher creatures.

The numbers on each grid space show you the total of the levels of the monsters in the adjacent squares. You can only attack monsters that have the same level as you or you'll lose HP. You gain experience points every time you kill a monster, and eventually you'll be able to go up a level and attack more monsters. In this way, you can slowly chip away at a grid, and finally kill every monster on it. You can also mark grid spaces with numbers to aid your progress.

There are different-sized grids and alternate modes to play, including Blind mode (a style of play more like *Minesweeper*) and Extreme mode (a mode with far more high-level monsters). A version of the game called *iMamono-Sweeper* is available for the iPhone.

http://indiegam.es/playMamono

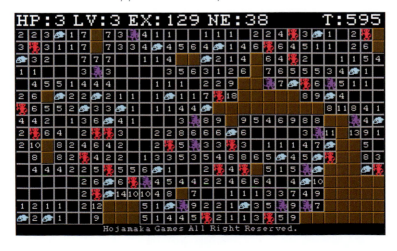

K.O.L.M.

Antony Lavelle

K.O.L.M. follows a robot who has lost all his parts. His mother isn't happy about it, and sends him out to retrieve them all so he can build himself back up. The game plays out in classic exploration-gaming style, with players collecting upgrades to open new pathways to explore.

The little robot can barely move at first, and the screen is blurred since his visual chip is missing. Throughout play you'll find parts that will allow him to walk, jump, shoot, duck, and perform many other useful actions. As the robot moves farther into the labyrinth, the action is shown on various CCTV cameras, which zoom in and out frequently to show the entire area. Eventually, you'll find enough parts to allow the robot to escape from his mysterious surroundings.

The game has been played roughly one million times and has been featured on a number of mainstream gaming sites, including the likes of PC Gamer and Rock Paper Shotgun.

http://indiegam.es/playKOLM

Robot Unicorn Attack

Spiritonin Media

Rainbows, unicorns, and harmony are the cornerstones of *Robot Unicorn Attack*, a fast-paced platformer with automatic running. All you need to worry about is jumping between the ledges and smashing through brightly-coloured stars to make your "wish" come true.

The unicorn is perpetually running towards the right, leaving a rainbow trail as it dashes along. You use the Z key to make it jump and then double jump, so that you can clear gaps and pursue your "wish." Along the way you'll need to use your X key to crash through stars, and dolphins will jump up from below as your score increases. The soundtrack is the icing on the cake—the song "Always" by British synthpop duo Erasure plays in the background and gives the game a fantastic atmosphere.

The game has proved incredibly popular, with over 35 million plays at the time of writing. There is also a Heavy Metal and a Christmas edition.

http://indiegam.es/playRUA

Loved

Alexander Ocias

Loved is a short platformer with an underlying art game feel. You control a chubby monster, and must decide whether to obey an unidentified voice that is constantly barking orders as you help the monster avoid spikes and other dangerous obstacles.

Over the course of the game, you can either give in to the rude voice's commands or disobey everything it says; the world that emerges will be shaped by what you do. If you follow its orders, the world will become more detailed but remain black and white—go against the voice, however, and colour will begin to emerge and give the whole experience a completely different feeling.

It's worth playing through the game twice to see how the world, the text, and the ending are altered by whether or not you decide to comply. There is also a secret area to be found for intrepid explorers.

http://indiegam.es/playLoved

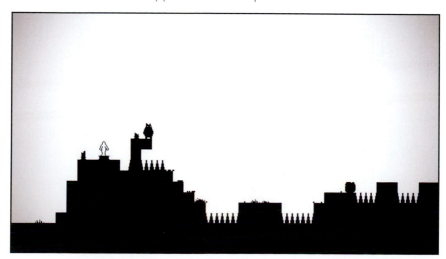

Vox Populi, Vox Dei

Weremsoft

Latin for "The voice of the people is the voice of God," *Vox Populi, Vox Dei* follows the brutal exploits of a ninja trying to save his ex-lover from the planet's dominant race: werewolves.

The hero can make himself invisible so that he can sneak up on the werewolves before he leaps through the air to drag the creatures to the ground. Once a werewolf is down, you hammer the space bar to rip the werewolf to shreds in a very bloody fashion. If a werewolf spots you before you strike, his chest will open up and a stream of bullets will fly out, knocking you to the ground instantly. The idea is to be as stealthy as possible and only use force when necessary, as you cannot move while on top of your opponent.

The sheer brutality of your character's actions compared to the werewolves' attacks may make you wonder who, exactly, is the enemy in this tale. There have been around two million online plays, and developer Weremsoft is currently working on a sequel.

http://indiegam.es/playVoxPopuli

Corporate Climber

Pixeljam Games

It takes hard work and dedication to earn a seat in the boardroom of a big corporation these days. *Corporate Climber* chronicles one man's climb from lowly janitor to suit-wearing bigwig—and then his swift fall from grace.

Starting in the basement, you'll need to complete silly challenges on each floor to get promoted and move up to the next level. Initially, you'll be fixing dangerous electrical wires and dodging rats, but eventually you'll be firing surplus staff and literally "cooking the books." Once he reaches the top, though, it all goes a little wrong for our hard-working hero and he suddenly finds himself headed in a different direction.

There are an assortment of special unlocks and endings in *Corporate Climber*, like the five alternative events that can occur on the top floor of the building, and a secret floor with all the lights turned off that can only be reached if the character is wearing a particular outfit when scaling the tower.

http://indiegam.es/playCC

Boondog

Matthew Hart

Harking back to the days of classic precision platformers such as *Flashback* and *Prince of Persia*, *Boondog* demands that you carefully consider each move that you make: a single incorrect leap, turn, or drop can end in disaster.

The hero doesn't have a huge range of moves you can play with—he can run, jump, hang, and push—yet every press of a button must be carefully considered. For example, he cannot fall a great distance, so instead of having him simply walk off a platform, you'll have to move him to the edge and then let him hang off the side before he drops. Once you've got your head around the game's mechanics, the puzzles will start to kick in, and you'll have buttons to press and barrels to push. Your goal is to reach the portal on each level, but this is easier said than done thanks to the clever and devious level design.

The game was originally released as a download title in 2008, but it was later ported to Flash by developer Miroslav Malesevic, so it can now be played on your web browser.

http://indiegam.es/playBoondog

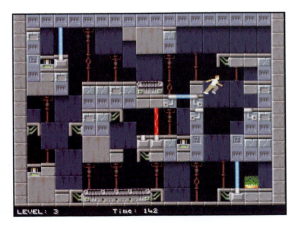

Boxgame

Sophie Houlden

In the three-dimensional world of Boxgame, it's hard to know which way is up. As you walk and jump around the perimeter of the game's giant translucent boxes, floors can become walls, walls can become ceilings, and players will become disoriented.

What happens depends on how you move around at the edges of the box. If you walk around the corner of two faces, you'll move around the box, but if you jump above or fall below the face you currently occupy, then gravity (and the faces of the cube) will shift. A host of clever puzzles play off this mind-bending concept (try moving through two different edges in a single jump!). Players who are looking for more of a challenge can look for hidden teddy bears on each level.

Boxgame was based on a student prototype called *Qb* that Sophie worked on with a team at her university. Having enjoyed working on developing the concept, she decided to take it in her own direction.

http://indiegam.es/playBoxgame

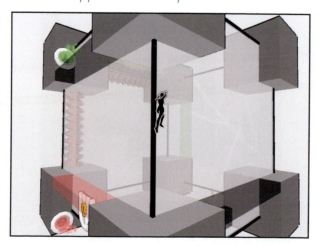

Shift

Antony Lavelle

The name *Shift* refers not only to the game's main puzzle mechanic, but also to the button you'll need to play the game. You are Subject 32763, and a series of black-and-white test rooms await your exploration.

You need to reach the exit door in each room to move on, but after the first few levels, the doors suddenly appear to be out of reach. This is where the "Shift" concept comes in—the main character has the ability to flip 180 degrees so you can move onto the floor, at which point the screen will rotate and you'll find yourself on the other side of the floor, giving you a whole new area to explore. You need to use this flipping tactic to solve a whole host of fiendish puzzles that will have you leaping over spikes and picking up keys.

The game has been played over 3.5 million times in total, and numerous sequels have been released, including a couple of editions for the iPhone.

http://indiegam.es/playShift

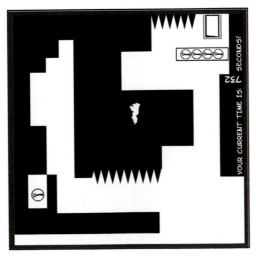

I Wish I Were the Moon

Daniel Benmergui

I Wish I Were the Moon is a short love story told in the form of a puzzle game. A girl paddles along in a boat beneath a beautiful night sky, all the while looking up at the moon—and the boy perched atop it.

You are tasked with finding all five possible endings to the game. Your only form of control is to click on the scene with your mouse, which allows you to take a snapshot of whatever you choose. You then click elsewhere to move whatever was in the snapshot—so, for example, you might want to take a photo of the boy and then drop him into the boat with the girl. It's tricky to find all five endings, as it requires that you consider all possible combinations.

The game was inspired by *The Distance of the Moon*, a short story from the book *Cosmicomics* by Italo Calvino. It was part of a collection of games called *Moon Stories* that were presented at the Tokyo Game Show during the Sense of Wonder Night.

http://indiegam.es/playIWIWTM

Maverick

John Cooney

In *Maverick,* you are a gunslinger in the wild—rather green—West. Since the hero cannot walk, he must instead use the momentum from firing his pistols rapidly to propel himself past numerous obstacles and dangers.

As you pass through each section of the world, more obstacles (such as cacti and spikes) will be added. There are also sections that require you to shoot down a crumbling wall to progress, which may be tricky given that shooting the wall will cause your character to be propelled in the opposite direction. Eventually, you'll also have to cope with gravity changes in the form of walls that become floors and gravity that disappears altogether. Every time the hero dies, a gravestone will be left in his place with a number on it to keep track of how many times he has bitten the dust.

If you manage to beat all 15 levels, there is a "magnificent magic pig" waiting for you with a present (although you may find that actually collecting the present is a little tricky).

http://indiegam.es/playMaverick

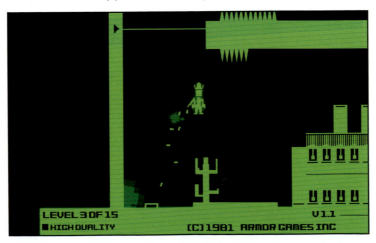

Cursor*10

Yoshio "Nekogames" Ishii

Ten mouse cursors must work together to reach the 16th floor of a tower. The twist is that you control only one cursor at a time, and must cooperate with previous versions of the pointer to proceed.

*Cursor*10* starts you off with a single mouse pointer that you use to click on the stairways and move up the tower. However, you'll eventually come across a room that you can't move past with a single mouse cursor, and at that point your current cursor's life will run out. When you start again at the bottom of the stairs with the second cursor, you'll notice cursor one springing into action and bolting up the stairs of the tower, moving in exactly the same way it did before. The goal is to arrange all the cursors so that the final one can reach the top and win the game.

A sequel, *Cursor*10 2nd Session*, is also available to play online; it offers a brand new tower to scale.

http://indiegam.es/playCursor10

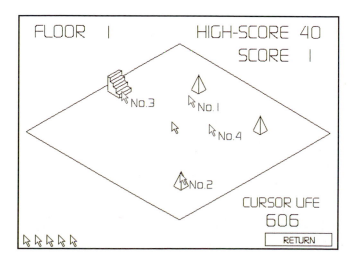

Give Up, Robot

Matt Thorson

Encouragement is overrated. In *Give Up, Robot* a sinister robotic voice constantly tells the bobbing hero to abandon his pointless voyage—and perhaps you should listen, as this game is seriously difficult!

Your robot can fire a grappling hook and latch onto surfaces to swing across chasms and obstacles. The first dozen levels aren't too taxing as you learn the different moves and discover the dangers that impede your progress. But when the harder levels kick in with their incredibly tricky areas to master, you'll soon begin to wonder whether the voice is right. And, as if the later levels aren't challenging enough, there's also a special hard mode for when you've completed the main set of levels.

With the game receiving more than 2.5 million plays, a sequel was bound to be in the works. *Give Up Robot 2* leaves the psychedelic backdrop and stifling voice behind, opting for more open areas and even more swinging fun.

http://indiegam.es/playGUR

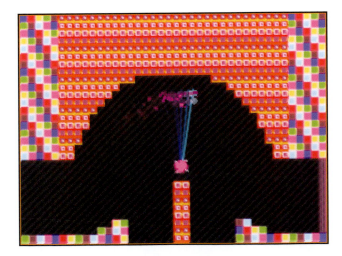

Where We Remain

Twofold Secret

Trapped on a mysterious, procedurally-generated island, you think only of finding your sweetheart who has been hidden away in one of the many dark and dangerous caves—and of evading the terrible beasts that roam the land outside the caves.

Where We Remain gives you few hints about how you are supposed to find your love again. You must figure out on your own how best to explore the land and find the items that will aid your progress, while you also investigate the caverns that are filled with shadows of yourself. Don't stand around thinking for too long, though, or terrifying clouds—shrieking in a most vile manner—will launch themselves at you. It's incredible how scary the game can feel when such simple sound effects break the eerie silence!

There are three endings, each dependent on how you go about finding your lost love, and multiple levels of difficulty for players who want a serious scare.

http://indiegam.es/playWWR

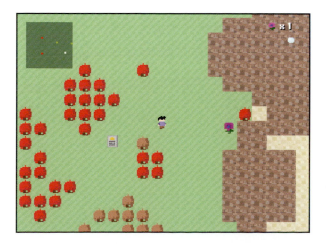

Part 3

Commercial Games

While the preceding 200 games have been completely free to play, this last 50 are downloads for purchase. Commercial indie games usually offer a lot more polish and content than their gratis counterparts, and are often much cheaper than your average big-budget release.

Some commercial indie developers use a "Pay What You Want" system—rather than putting a set value on their work, these developers ask you to choose whatever price you want to pay. Every title featured here is available to download for PC, but may also be available for other platforms including Mac, the Nintendo Wii, the Xbox 360 and the Playstation 3. It will be clearly stated whenever this is the case.

Squid Yes! Not So Octopus!

Robert "Oddbob" Fearon

Squid Yes! Not So Octopus! is a series of arena shooters that revel in big flashy explosions and utter chaos. You are a squid who fires laser beams out of his head as he battles the aliens attacking his planet.

The squid can only shoot in the direction that he is facing, hence he'll need to quickly move away from the oncoming hordes and then reverse direction, rushing towards them with laser fire blazing. Enemies will explode with bright, extravagant colours and it'll soon become very difficult to see where you're going. If you can last long enough, the aliens will finally retreat, leaving you to celebrate your victory.

Developer Robert Fearon has put together a "Bundle of Wrong" on his website that gives you access to all his games, which you can purchase for whatever price you like. The collection includes all the *SYNSO* games and even some titles he's still working on.

http://indiegam.es/playSYNSO

World of Goo

2D Boy

The World of Goo Corporation has disturbed the docile Goo Balls of the land by laying a strange pipe system to suck them all up. But the Goo Balls are curious little things, and can't help taking a peek inside the pipes.

Your objective is to connect some of the Goo together to create sturdy structures like towers and bridges that the remaining Balls can use to reach the pipe on each level. Gradually, different types of Goo Balls will be introduced and you'll need to be clever about where you place the Goo. All the Goo Balls you've collected can then be used to create a huge tower in the corporation complex that reaches high into the sky, and your tower can be ranked online along with those created by other World of Goo players.

World of Goo won two Independent Games Festival awards in 2008, and versions are available for PC, Mac, the Nintendo Wii, and the iPad. Kyle Gabler and Ron Carmel of 2D Boy ran a weeklong "Pay-What-You-Want" sale for the game's first birthday—a promotion technique that has since become common in the indie game world.

http://indiegam.es/playWorldofGoo

VVVVVV

Terry Cavanagh

VVVVVV is a retro platformer with a unique twist. Pronounced "Vee," the game features a main character who cannot jump, but who can flip upside down and walk on the ceiling. *VVVVVV*'s level design is built around this special mechanic, presenting players with an original way in which to dodge opponents and the game's ever-present spikes as they navigate the complex rooms.

Captain Veridian must search Dimension VVVVVV to find his five missing crewmates. He soon finds out that each of *VVVVVV*'s levels comes with its own set of environmental idiosyncrasies: like "The Tower," which has the screen continually scrolling upwards, and "The Laboratory," which features inversion planes that will cause him to flip in mid-air.

Reportedly, *VVVVVV*'s name comes from the fact that the names of the six main characters all start with the letter V . . . but many players attribute it to the huge number of spikes in the game (and the name looks like a set of upside-down spikes).

http://indiegam.es/playVVVVVV

Braid

Jonathan Blow

Perhaps one of the best-known indie games of recent years, *Braid* follows Tim as he tries to rescue his princess from a terrible monster. Tim's ability to manipulate time will certainly serve him well on his quest.

Using this power, he can move back to a previous moment and even bring himself back from the dead. As he progresses through the chapters, he finds areas and objects that are not affected by his powers, but in situations where he wants to alter the past while keeping certain other elements unchanged, this can be used to his advantage. Jigsaw puzzle pieces are scattered around the world, and Tim must collect these to open up the final chapter and find his missing sweetheart.

Braid was the winner of the Innovation in Game Design Award at the Independent Games Festival in 2006, and was eventually released on the Xbox 360, Playstation 3, PC, and Mac. Many of the game's platforming elements borrow from the classic *Super Mario Brothers* formula, but gameplay will cause you to question your understanding of the seemingly similar mechanics.

http://indiegam.es/playBraid

Lunnye Devitsy

Boss Baddie

A small, moon-dwelling creature has fallen to Earth and wants to find its way home. *Lunnye Devitsy* (translated roughly as "Moon Girls" in Russian) follows the creature's peculiar, pixelated ascent through the night sky.

Your alien protagonist must explore Earth to find the things it needs to get home, even diving deep beneath the surface to solve puzzles and collect the necessary upgrades. You cannot be killed and therefore *Lunnye Devitsy* is a relaxing experience rather than an action-packed one. There are six different methods for reaching the moon—some require that you simply explore, while others involve collecting parts of a machine that can be used to propel you to the stars.

The game was developed as a celebration of the first moon landings, which occurred just over 40 years ago when *Lunnye Devitsy* was released. Developer Boss Baddie also has a "Lunar Pack" for sale that includes both *Lunnye Devitsy* and another atmospheric game called *Wake*.

http://indiegam.es/playLunnye

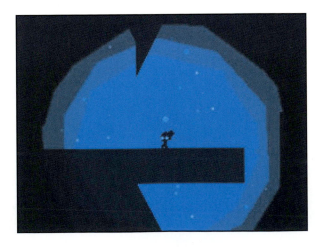

The Path

Tale of Tales

Based loosely on the fairy tale *Little Red Riding Hood, The Path* is a horror game that explores various life experiences through the eyes of children. One by one, you play six girls who travel down a path to visit their grandmother.

The game begins with the girl you've chosen standing at the beginning of a path that winds through a forest. Only one instruction is given: "Go to grandmother's house and stay on the path." If you follow this rule, you will visit your grandmother as planned and the game will be over. However, if you stray from the path, you'll encounter a whole host of surreal, creepy situations and experiences. A different narrative goes with each girl, and several of the storylines are rather disturbing.

When *The Path* was released for PC and Mac in 2009, it caused much controversy amongst the press and gamers alike, but it also picked up awards for best sound and best design at the Spanish hóPLAY International Video Game Festival.

http://indiegam.es/playThePath

NightSky

Nicklas "Nifflas" Nygren

When the sun is setting on the distant horizon, it's time to get the ball rolling. *NightSky* gives players a sphere to control and hundreds of wonderful physics-based puzzles to overcome.

The ball can be rolled left and right, but there's far more to it than that. On each set of levels, the sphere takes on a couple of special powers that will help you roll on. Perhaps you'll be able to zoom rapidly over ramps, or invert gravity and stick to the ceiling—discovering abilities and experimenting with the surroundings is half the fun! The level design is solid throughout, and the gorgeous backdrops make *NightSky* a real treat for the eyes.

The game went through various name changes, including *Skymning* and *Night Game*, before developer Nicklas Nygren settled on *NightSky*. In development for nearly four years, the game is available for PC and Mac, with a Nintendo Wii version in the works at the time of writing.

http://indiegam.es/playNightSky

Arvoesine

Alastair John Jack

With its old-school visuals, simple interface, and tough gameplay, *Arvoesine* is a homage to the classic NES platformers of the '80s. You are a Roman soldier launching spears at his foes and slashing his sword at anything that comes within range.

The spears fly in an arc; therefore, the timing of your throws is crucial if you want to hit the target. If your adversaries manage to slip past the spears, the hero's trusty blade will chop them down in an instant. Certain bad guys will give you a taste of your own medicine by firing projectiles in your direction, but they'll be no match for your shield. At the end of each level, you'll come up against some form of mythological being that must be destroyed before you are able to progress.

Arvoesine is rather short, with only five levels to battle your way through. However, multiple playthroughs will reveal a clever scoring system that's based on how many swings you take to kill each enemy. Once you realize this, you'll have even more fun by trying to grab the highest scores possible. *Arvoesine* is available for PC download.

http://indiegam.es/playArvoesine

And Yet It Moves

Broken Rules

Named after a phrase supposedly uttered by Italian philosopher Galileo, *And Yet It Moves* is a platformer with a literal twist. Whenever the main character comes across a wall blocking his path, you can simply rotate the world until the wall becomes the floor.

As the protagonist runs through this bizarre land made out of ripped pieces of paper, you can spin his surroundings to alter the direction of gravity. Not only will the hero be affected, but any objects or creatures in the vicinity will also be pulled downwards. With this in mind, it's possible to build the hero's momentum up as he continues to fall through space, although his days are numbered if he hits the ground at any speed.

And Yet It Moves is available for PC, Mac, and the Nintendo Wii. The Wii-Ware version is particularly interesting, as you control the protagonist's rotation by turning the Wii Remote.

http://indiegam.es/playAYIM

AaaaaAAaaaAAAaaAAAAaAAAAA!!!
A Reckless Disregard for Gravity

Dejobaan Games

If you're wondering how the name of this game is pronounced, imagine someone screaming while jumping from a very tall building. Indeed, the game is all about base jumping from huge structures and trying not to smash your face on too many obstacles on the way down.

As you fall at top speed, a variety of bizarre dangers and floating skyscrapers will litter your path. Float close to any of these objects to "kiss" it and you'll earn big points for bravery. Now and again you'll catch spectators watching from the ground, and you can wave to your fans or flip off protesters. Later levels feature even more surreal obstacles to dodge around—along with city buildings to graffiti, birds to slam into, and needles to thread. Just remember to deploy your parachute before you hit the ground!

Aaaaa! is available for PC. Dejobaan Games is currently working on a spiritual sequel to the game called *1... 2... 3... KICK IT! (Drop That Beat Like an Ugly Baby),* which will combine the freefalling concept with a music game.

http://indiegam.es/playAaaaa

Time Gentlemen, Please!

Zombie Cow Studios

Inspired by classic LucasArts adventure games such as *Monkey Island* and *Sam and Max*, *Time Gentlemen, Please!* follows the exploits of moronic duo Ben and Dan as they accidentally wipe out the entire human race, then go back in time to fix their mistakes.

As you'd expect, they actually make things a whole lot worse, and Hitler has soon taken over the world with his army of Nazi dinosaurs. The humour is very crude, very British, and very hilarious throughout as Ben and Dan continue to travel through time, solving puzzles and getting themselves into the most peculiar of situations. Items can be collected in one time period and carried into another, and environments range from the time of cavemen to futuristic surroundings packed with robots.

Time Gentlemen, Please! is a sequel to free-to-play *Ben There, Dan That*, the first Ben and Dan adventure. It's not necessary to play the first game to fully enjoy the second, and both are available for PC download.

http://indiegam.es/playTGP

Irukandji

Charlie's Games

An Irukandji is a type of jellyfish, so it's not surprising to find that the main character in this game is rather squid-like. Your mission is to blast any sea monsters that cross your path as you swim through an underwater trench.

Each creature in *Irukandji* is procedurally animated, as is the gorgeous glowing ambience. The entire game is really a feast for the eyes, with beautiful explosions of neon colour and lovely particle effects. As you destroy your opponents, you collect power-ups that will boost your laser fire until you are a serious force to be reckoned with. Don't get too complacent, however, as the giant crab boss at the end is far from a pushover.

Irukandji has only one short level to play through, but there are six different jellyfish to control and each has its own unique firing pattern and individual online scoreboard. Available for PC and Mac, you can pay whatever price you want for the game.

http://indiegam.es/playIrukandji

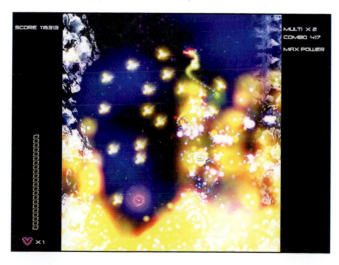

Mr. Robot

Moonpod

The interstellar-colony ship Eidolon has hundreds of cryogenically frozen humans on board, ready to begin new lives on the planet Prime. Unfortunately, the ship's supercomputer malfunctions during the voyage and puts all of those lives at risk.

A lowly service robot called Asimov steps up to save the day. Asimov must override the computer's lockdown mode by solving puzzles, while at the same time evading crazed security bots. One half of the game involves jumping between platforms, flipping switches, and pushing boxes to progress; the other sees you hacking into terminals and fighting enemies via turn-based RPG action. Bits of energy called Energon can also be collected to earn cash and boost Asimov's health.

Mr. Robot also comes with a handy level editor for creating your own scenarios, and leaderboards for tracking your progress. A PC version is available for purchase.

http://indiegam.es/playMrRobot

The Thrill of Combat

Mark "Messhof" Essen

The Thrill of Combat is quite possibly one of the most disorientating experiences you'll ever have, even though the concept sounds simple (if a little bizarre): fly your helicopter into enemy territory, kill the soldiers, cut out their vital organs—and repeat.

Your first 15 minutes, however, will be spent trying to maintain control over the helicopter and keeping it from crashing every few seconds. As your vehicle pitches forward and backward, so will the camera angle, creating an incredibly nauseating effect. Once you've managed to kill a couple of soldiers, dropping your gunner down to cut their organs out will be a whole different ball game, as you attempt to use your mouse to slice perfectly around each organ while at the same time keeping control of the helicopter. The pieces you collect get dumped back at your boat.

The PC game is designed for two players, with one person controlling the helicopter while the other shoots and cuts, but a single player can do both. A free browser game called *Party Boat* that features elements from *The Thrill of Combat* is also available.

http://indiegam.es/playTOC

Brainpipe

Digital Eel

Take a trip into your subconscious with *Brainpipe* and find the Unhumanity Glyph, an ancient relic that will grant you the ability to trade your body in for a new alien form. If you're looking for a trippy, psychedelic experience, you've come to the right place.

As you travel down the Brainpipe, different obstacles will block your way that must be evaded by using your mouse. When the velocity ramps up, left click will become your best friend by slowing the action down for a moment so you can catch your breath and assess the situation. The visuals change constantly during play, going from bright, bouncy colours one moment to dark and eerie the next. Freaky groaning noises play as you career down this mental tunnel.

Make sure to grab the glowing glyphs and avoid the enemies along the way, else your journey to enlightenment will be cut short. Winner of the Excellence In Audio Award at the 2009 Independent Games Festival, *Brainpipe* is available for PC and Mac download.

http://indiegam.es/playBrainpipe

Bit.Trip Beat

Gaijin Games

Bit.Trip Beat is the first title in a series of tough rhythm games. With a resemblance to the classic arcade game *Pong*, the game requires you to stop coloured cubes from leaving the screen on the left-hand side by knocking them back with a paddle.

The cubes do not approach randomly, however—they move in time with the music and arrive level with your paddle at each beat. As the tempo of the soundtrack ramps up, the cubes will come thick and fast, and you'll need quick reactions, a steady hand, and a good sense of rhythm to ensure that every cube is caught. If you miss too many in quick succession, both the visuals and the music will devolve and make the game look and sound exactly like the '70s table tennis classic.

There are six *Bit.Trip* games in total, each featuring a character called Commander Video who was part of the original viral marketing for the series. *Bit.Trip Beat* has PC, Mac, Nintendo Wii, and iPhone versions available for purchase.

http://indiegam.es/playBTB

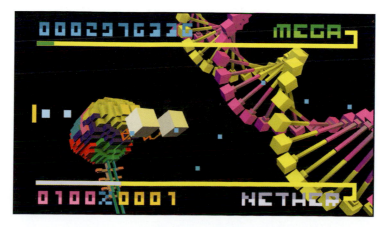

Delve Deeper

Lunar Giant Studios

With your band of dwarven adventurers on the prowl for precious rubies and gems, those abandoned mines full to the brim with incredible wealth and lost treasures aren't going to stay deserted for long. *Delve Deeper* is a quirky turn-based race to gather up as much gold as possible before the teams competing against you manage to line their pockets first.

Each turn consists of digging deeper into the mountain, then guiding your dwarfs and their pickaxes to the nearest treasure. However, the competing teams are not your only worry—terrible monsters also lurk in the depths of the earth, and whenever a horde of creatures manages to enter your caverns, they'll home straight in on your team. Yet monsters are not always a hindrance, as you can purposely lead beasts into your opponents' camps to wreak havoc and buy you valuable time.

Up to four players can take each other on via hotseat play on the same computer, or a single player can compete against AI-controlled teams. *Delve Deeper* is available for PC.

http://indiegam.es/playDelveDeeper

Rocketbirds: Revolution!

Ratloop Asia

The evil Penguin Empire has captured the city of Albatropolis, and a hero is desperately needed to remove the threat and free the civilians. Enter Hardboiled, a veteran Cock of War who jets in to kill El Putzki, leader of the Penguins.

Rocketbirds: Revolution! crosses elements of the classic platformer *Flashback* with the *Oddworld* puzzle series. Hardboiled must run, leap, and shoot his way from behind enemy lines to accomplish his mission—although for the most part, stealth is his best friend. There are an assortment of puzzles to solve along the way, and you'll have to have quick reactions to take down your adversaries before they get a shot in your direction. The game is brimming with personality thanks to gorgeous backdrops and animations, not to mention a slick intro video.

Currently available for PC and Mac as a paid browser game, a special, updated version of *Revolution!* is also in the works. *Rocketbirds: Reloaded!* is coming to the Playstation 3 and PC, and will take the feedback received from players of the original game to expand and improve the concept.

http://indiegam.es/playRocketbirds

Flotilla

Blendo Games

Have you ever fought against an armada of penguin bandits in the depths of space? Probably not, but have no fear—turn-based strategy game *Flotilla* is here to fill that void, providing oodles of strategic gameplay in a distinctly bizarre universe.

Presented with a randomly populated arena, you're tasked with sending your fleet to crush the opposition. It's not that simple, though, as the enemy ships will only be damaged if they're hit from below or from the rear. Consequently, you must position your ships so that they're flanking the enemy, but at least you'll have a three-dimensional area to soar through. Each new adventure is different, and features zany adversaries like crazed hippos and chicken pirates, which are positioned differently each time.

The single-player campaign features multiple upgrades for your flotilla and online leaderboards to scale. Grab a friend, and you can either play through the campaign cooperatively or destroy each other in a head-to-head Skirmish battle. *Flotilla* can be downloaded for both PC and the Xbox 360.

http://indiegam.es/playFlotilla

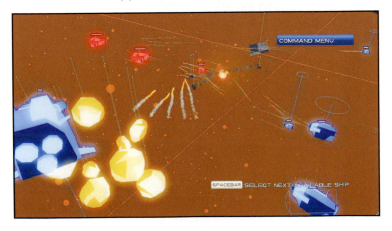

Windosill

Vectorpark

Windosill is a magical voyage of exploration, during which the key to progression is simply playing around with your surroundings. Over a series of ten rooms, you're presented with experimental play toys that must be solved in order to move your little chugging car along.

Each room is even more surreal than the last, with strange creatures and abstract objects to touch, pull, and drag around the screen. *Windosill* is a calming sort of puzzler in that you are left to find the solutions to each scenario at your own pace, and each absurd environment is brimming with personality and colour. Once you've managed to find the small white cube, you place it in a gap above the small door so that your strange blocky car can continue on its journey.

The first half of *Windosill* is completely free to play online. To access the second half, you'll need to pay a small sum to obtain an activation code.

http://indiegam.es/playWindosill

Grappling Hook

Speed Run Games

You're trapped in a series of metal chambers in space, and your only means of escape is your trusty laser grappling hook. Aim and fire it at any green surface to launch your hook in that direction, then either hold it to stay put, or let go and use the momentum to soar over danger.

Presented from a first-person perspective and similar in style to classic action puzzler *Portal, Grappling Hook* oozes with creativity and provides hours of exciting quick-draw gameplay. Some situations will require that you fire the hook rapidly and cling to the ceiling to avoid death, while others will force you to take a leap of faith by diving to your (apparent) doom and hooking onto a panel at the last moment. You'll need lots of precision-timed shots to survive, especially in the later levels.

Each of the 31 levels has special challenges to complete, such as achieving perfect runs and reaching a goal in a set amount of time. There's even a level editor to create your own impossible runs. *Grappling Hook* is available for purchase in both PC and Mac versions.

http://indiegam.es/playGrappling

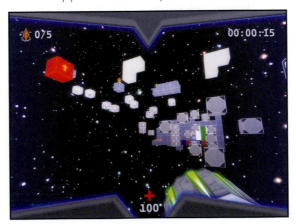

Trials 2: Second Edition

Redlynx

Trials 2: Second Edition makes riding a real motorbike look like a walk in the park. The goal seems simple: finish the race without toppling over. But with the series of tough courses *Trials* throws at you, this is easier said than done.

Players use the arrow keys to balance the bike, accelerate over jumps (carefully!), and hop over obstacles. The game is set on a two-dimensional plane, with a variety of boxes, makeshift ramps, and fire barrels to navigate around. Every time the bike slips and the rider's head hits the floor, you'll hear a crunching noise; the rider's body will then curl up in various entertaining ways before you're sent back to the last checkpoint. With dozens of tracks, global high scores, multiple gameplay modes, and tracked statistics, there's lots of replay value to be found in this game.

The original game, *Trials*, provided the inspiration for this very polished outfit (you can still play the original online for free). *Trials 2: Second Edition* is available for PC, and there is also a version of the game for the Xbox 360 called *Trials HD*.

http://indiegam.es/playTrials2

Audiosurf

Dylan Fitterer

Forget *Guitar Hero* and *Rock Band*—*Audiosurf* is the true way to play along with your music collection. The game reads whatever mp3 file you feed into it, and creates a rollercoaster-style highway for you to cruise.

The type of level you get is determined by the pitch, tempo, and volume of your selected track. Faster, louder songs will get you a ride that spirals downwards at full force, while softer pieces will give you a smoother trip. As your ship zips along the track, coloured blocks will appear; if you collect three or more of the same colour, you'll empty the gauge and bag some hard-earned points.

There are various kinds of ships, and each will give you a different game-play experience by altering the rules of play. There's also a two-player co-op mode. *Audiosurf* was a huge success at the 2008 Independent Games Festival, winning both the Excellence In Audio and the Audience Awards. The game is available for PC, and a free version called *Audiosurf Tilt* is available from the Zune Marketplace.

http://indiegam.es/playAudiosurf

Downfall

Harvester Games

When Joe and Ivy Davis check in to the Quiet Haven hotel during a storm, they have no idea that they'll soon be facing a night of horror. Joe wakes to find Ivy missing, and the situation starts getting very twisted.

Downfall puts you in the shoes of an anxious and frightened Joe as he attempts to find his wife, and there are dark secrets and bloody scenes to be found every step of the way. In true adventure game style, you can interact with objects in each room and collect useful items that you utilize elsewhere to progress. With more than 70 hand-drawn areas to explore, and a chilling soundtrack to accompany the terror, *Downfall* is a mature adventure that will give you the creeps long after you quit the game.

At certain intervals during play, you'll be given options about what to do next, and your choices will determine the final ending that you receive. *Downfall* is a PC-only download.

http://indiegam.es/playDownfall

Super Meat Boy

Edmund McMillen and Tommy Refenes

Meat Boy's girlfriend has been kidnapped by the evil Doctor Fetus, leaving our fearless, meaty hero to hotfoot his way through worlds full of spinning blades, deadly acid, and the occasional vat of salt.

Meat Boy can run, jump, dodge, weave, and spring from wall to wall in the hope of reaching Bandage Girl at the end of each level, but more often than not he'll miscalculate when he makes a leap and end up in the grinder. Fortunately, Meat Boy is a resilient sort of guy, and he'll immediately be ready to tackle the level all over again. *Super Meat Boy* is an incredibly challenging game that throws seemingly impossible challenges your way constantly, and there is no better feeling than completing a particularly difficult level.

The game features a serious amount of content, with over 300 levels to play (these include hidden "warp zones" and "minus worlds"). The Xbox version has extra chapters added periodically, and the PC and Mac editions come with a level editor, which will allow players to create their own fiendish creations for others to download.

http://indiegam.es/playSMB

Machinarium

Amanita Design

You'd think that being taken apart and dumped on a scrapheap would spell the end for a robot, but our hero Josef has other plans. After reassembling his body and assessing the situation, he heads off to the city to seek his fortune.

Machinarium is a point-and-click adventure game that follows Josef as he attempts to overthrow a plot to blow up the city. The robots of this world cannot talk, but instead communicate via whistling, grunting, and other humorous noises. The game is bursting with personality, and includes gorgeous hand-drawn scenes and characters, and endearing animations. There are lots of different kinds of puzzles to solve too, from working out combinations of button presses to using items in the correct areas.

Machinarium won the Excellence In Visual Art Award at the 2009 Independent Games Festival and was released on PC and Mac. Developer Amanita Design is also hoping to release the game on the Nintendo Wii and Playstation 3.

http://indiegam.es/playMachinarium

Minecraft

Mojang

Recognised as one of the most successful and important indie games ever created, *Minecraft* is the vision of Swedish developer Markus "Notch" Persson. Players are given the opportunity to begin whatever adventure they see fit in its blocky world, and there's an option to play online with friends and craft a world together.

In this randomly-generated sandbox land, blocks can be broken down and used to build huge structures or be crafted into useful tools such as pickaxes, shovels, and weaponry. You can choose to create a home and model the surrounding areas as you like, or go on an epic journey where you'll dig deep into the ground to look for hidden treasures. As night falls, nasty creatures will come out to play and threaten whatever you've created.

At the time of writing, *Minecraft* was still in beta form, with a full release planned for sometime in 2011. Over one million copies of the game have been sold so far, and numerous communities and forums have popped up to assist players in their adventures.

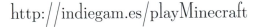

http://indiegam.es/playMinecraft

Nimbus

Noumenon Games

It's not often that puzzle and racing genres are combined in a game, but then again, it's not often you come across a game like *Nimbus*. Players quickly navigate a small bouncing craft around a series of mazes, keeping the vessel aloft and gaining momentum by bumping into walls.

The bouncy surfaces and handy cannons scattered around each level help greatly in reaching the goal. It's never simple, however, with a multitude of spike traps and huge rolling balls ready to bring your journey abruptly to a halt. The racing element comes in when you complete a level, and your time is ranked against other people around the world. Finding shortcuts and shaving seconds off your time is the key to reaching those number one spots.

Clever puzzles and entertaining, fast-paced level design provide the fun, while online scoreboards, hidden coins, and unlockable ships keep you coming back for more. *Nimbus* is available to purchase for PC.

Recettear: An Item Shop's Tale

EasyGameStation and Carpe Fulgur

Take a glimpse into the life of an RPG-item shopkeeper with *Recettear*, a satirical take on the RPG genre. A young girl called Recette is visited by a loan shark fairy and forced to open up an item shop in order to pay off a rather large debt.

The girl doesn't have many items to sell, and so must acquire the services of an adventurer who can enter dungeons full of nasty creatures and bring back tasty loot. Recette can then pack her shelves with wares in the hope that her punters will empty their wallets. The game successfully combines an adventuring style of play with shop management, and completes the package with a host of loveable characters and a very funny storyline.

Available for PC, *Recettear* was originally released by Japanese developer EasyGameStation but later translated into English by localization company Carpe Fulgur. More than 100,000 copies have been sold.

http://indiegam.es/playRecettear

The Blackwell Legacy

Wadjet Eye Games

Rosangela Blackwell and Joey Mallone are an unlikely but well-suited duo, given that Rosa is a medium and Joey is no longer living. Together they investigate supernatural goings-on and help tormented spirits move on to the afterlife.

The Blackwell Legacy is the first in a series of *Blackwell* games, and follows a mysterious series of suicides at a local university. Rosa and Joey are soon playing detective, speaking to the dead and unravelling exactly what is going on. Both characters are controlled separately and have their own special abilities—Joey is invisible, which allows him to spy on people, while Rosa can converse with suspects and witnesses. The story-based adventure feels very grown-up, with clever dialogue and an exciting plot.

There are currently three games in the *Blackwell* series, and *Blackwell Unbound* and *The Blackwell Convergence* provide even more ghostly detective work. All three are available for PC, and can be bought together in a special Blackwell Bundle.

http://indiegam.es/playBlackwell

Caster

Mike "Elecorn" Smith

Giving a rookie soldier the task of destroying an entire army doesn't sound like the greatest of plans. But this rookie isn't just any new recruit—this is a Caster soldier, whose high-speed blasts of energy can demolish anything in their path.

As the Flanx army storms across the plains of Middon, *Caster*'s hero must rush in and annihilate every soldier on the battlefield. As the enemy is destroyed, you'll receive energy that can be used to upgrade your powers and provide new abilities. This game is all about feeling insanely powerful, and as you destroy whole plots of land in one fell swoop, it will be hard to deny that you're a force to be reckoned with.

Caster is available for PC, Mac, and the iPhone. One-man development team Mike Smith promises new episodes to come, and any additional content released will be free for anyone who purchased the original game.

http://indiegam.es/playCaster

Auditorium

Cipher Prime

The music swells to a crescendo, but it requires a little direction to reach its full potential. In *Auditorium,* you are tasked with manipulating streams of sound into audio containers so that the gorgeous music will be released to reverberate in your eardrums.

You have a number of tools at your disposal to help you with your work, ranging from arrows that alter the flow of the sound waves to repelling effects that will push the sound away from whatever area you choose. As you guide the flow of sound into an audio container, the music will begin to play quietly, and eventually the volume will rise as the container is filled to the top. Sound-streams of different colours are introduced as you progress through the chapters, leading to much tougher puzzles and solutions.

Auditorium is a Flash game that is played on your web browser, thus it works with both PC and Mac. An iPhone version has also been released; a trial version is available that allows you to play the first chapter for free.

http://indiegam.es/playAuditorium

Sleep Is Death (Geisterfahrer)

Jason Rohrer

Geisterfahrer is German for "Ghost Driver," which is an apt description for the two-player storyteller *Sleep Is Death*. One player takes part in a story as if it were an adventure game, while the other manipulates the scene, characters, and dialogue to create his or her own world.

The action is turn-based and alternates between "the player" and "the controller." The player moves the hero around, talks to other characters, and in general performs whatever acts seem appropriate. The controller is then given 30 seconds in which to prepare the follow-up scene, continuing conversations and drawing any necessary visuals on the fly. The player can either choose to follow along with the story the controller has created or attempt to break out of the confines of the script and force new angles.

Sleep Is Death is available for PC and Mac at whatever price you are willing to pay. Since the game is a two-player experience, two copies of the game are provided with each purchase.

http://indiegam.es/playSID

Leave Home

Hermitgames

Leaving home for the first time is never easy, especially when you're an abstract, laser-firing burst of light. Fortunately for *Leave Home* players, the world alters itself depending on how well—or badly—you play.

If you're good with your shots, kill plenty of enemies, and generally survive for a fair amount of time, this horizontal shooter will up the ante and throw tougher bad guys your way at a much higher frequency. But die multiple times in a row and you'll find that the hostiles will go easy on you. *Leave Home* uses a special difficulty system that's dynamic, meaning that the longer you stay alive, the harder the game becomes. During five-minute play sessions the game may also yank your ship out of the current scenario and dump you into another random situation without warning.

Each playthrough will yield different outcomes, which leads to a serious amount of replayability. *Leave Home* can be downloaded for PC and the Xbox 360.

http://indiegam.es/playLeaveHome

Darwinia

Introversion Software

When a mad scientist creates a digital world full of polygonal people, it's probably only a matter of time before deadly viruses find their way into the system. *Darwinia* puts you in charge of destroying the bugs and saving the tribe.

A number of different units—accessed via drawing gestures with your mouse—are available to players. Each level contains buildings that need to be captured and viruses that need to be killed. When you destroy a bug in the system, you'll receive Soul points that can be used to spawn more Darwinians to support your cause. Eventually, you'll witness huge battles between your soldiers and the various viruses infecting your virtual playground.

Darwinia took home three prizes from the 2006 Independent Games Festival, including the Seumas McNally Grand Prize, and both PC and Mac versions are available for sale. An online multiplayer edition called *Multiwinia* is also downloadable, and *Darwinia+* for the Xbox 360 includes both editions in a complete package.

http://indiegam.es/playDarwinia

Eversion

Guilherme S Tows (aka Zaratustra Productions)

In *Eversion* you are a happy-go-lucky flower called Zee Tee, prancing through a cute world full of smiling enemies and precious gems as you carry out a quest to save the Princess. Consequently, you may be surprised when you learn that *Eversion* is also an incredibly creepy game.

Play is heavily inspired by the classic *Super Mario* titles, with simple plat-forming mechanics. However, there's a twist: whenever you come across an obstacle blocking your path, there's an option to stand between two flowers and "everse"—that is, hie yourself to another reality in which (hopefully) that obstacle is missing. As you move more deeply into the various realities, you'll find that the world is no longer cutesy and happy; far from it, in fact. Without revealing too much, let's just say that the words "dark" and "grim" come to mind.

There are three different endings, and the one you get will depend on how many gems you collect during play. There is a free edition of *Eversion* avail-able for download, although the commercial version features high-definition visuals and some altered level design. Both versions are PC-only.

http://indiegam.es/playeversion

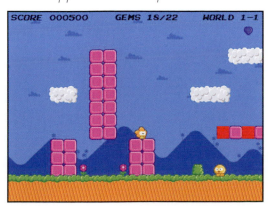

Osmos

Hemisphere Games

It's survival of the biggest in the chilled-out world of *Osmos*. You control a round organism floating through space, and smaller motes that collide with you will be swallowed up by your mass—but any larger ones you touch will feast on you instead! AI-generated motes will even hunt you down or scamper away to stay alive.

Keeping the balance of power in your favour is tricky, thanks to your only means of gaining momentum: ejecting matter. Doing so will propel your mote in any direction you choose, but obviously you'll also shrink slightly. *Osmos*'s procedurally-populated worlds test your ability to change tactics on the fly constantly, and multiple game modes provide additional puzzle, action, and strategy elements.

Osmos won the Direct2Drive Vision Award at the 2009 Independent Games Festival, and soon afterwards it was released for PC and Mac. Touch-screen editions for the iPhone and the iPad were later made available.

http://indiegam.es/playOsmos

The Oil Blue

Vertigo Games

In the near future, the world's reliance on oil is at an all-time high and drilling company United Oil of Oceana is raking the money in. You are an officer on one of its ships, whose mission it is to scour the ocean for abandoned oil-drilling islands and claim them for United Oil.

The Oil Blue is a multitasking bonanza in which you attempt to keep an assortment of satisfyingly clunky drilling machines running simultaneously. Some machines will only need you to press a button or two every now and then, while others will require much more care and attention to get the most out of them. If you work a machine too hard you'll need to perform maintenance to get it back in full working order again. The placement of islands is randomly generated, and a certain amount of the sticky stuff must be pumped on each in order for players to progress.

Dedication to the cause will be rewarded handsomely, as both you and your machines will level up based on how well you're playing. You'll also need to watch the stock market, and sell your oil at the best possible moment. *The Oil Blue* is a PC-only download.

http://indiegam.es/playTheOilBlue

Shatter

Sidhe Interactive

At first glance, *Shatter* appears to be just another *Breakout* clone, but it's far more than that. The objectives are familiar—keep the ball from leaving the arena by blocking its path with your paddle, and destroy all the blocks—but that's where the similarities end.

The ship you control can blow out and suck in, altering not only the course of the ball but also the movement of the blocks. If a block falls down and hits the paddle, you'll be disabled briefly, which is dangerous if the ball is en route to the gutter. As blocks are removed, crystals will scatter around the play area and can be sucked into the paddle. Collect enough of the crystals and you'll be able to unleash a devastating Shard Storm, allowing you to slow down time and fire a stream of bullets across the screen.

Shatter is incredibly stylish, with gorgeous visual effects and a solid, techno-pop soundtrack. Download is available for either PC or your Playstation 3.

http://indiegam.es/playShatter

Eufloria

Alex May and Rudolf Kremers

Sometimes the most simple and minimalist ideas can provide the most beautiful experiences. *Eufloria* is set in a world filled with perfectly round asteroids and flowers, and your objective is to send your seeds out and claim the world for your own.

Seeds spawn from each plant that you control, and will bury themselves into the soil on other asteroids. Once enough seeds have been planted, the comet becomes yours—but you'll also need to keep it heavily guarded from enemy-seedling armies. When you launch an attack on an opponent's asteroid, the different coloured seeds will do battle, firing tiny lasers at each other until one army is victorious.

Eufloria was originally designed for the TIGSource Procedural Generation competition under the name *Dyson* (after the Dyson tree hypothesis, which suggests that fractal-like plants can grow on meteorites). The game is available on PC, with releases for the Playstation 3, Mac, and iPhone planned for 2011.

http://indiegam.es/playEufloria

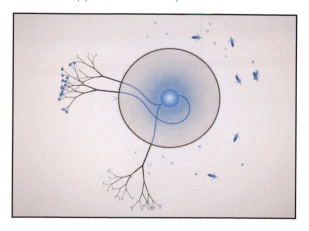

Aquaria

Bit Blot

Naija is a mermaid-like creature living a life of solitude deep beneath the sea. But one day a mysterious figure appears, and causes Naija to recall a stream of memories that had been locked away in her mind.

With these flashbacks propelling her on, Naija sets off through the gorgeous underwater world of *Aquaria* to discover the full truth. You control her movement and abilities entirely via the mouse (although keyboard-support is also available), and can explore the surroundings in a non-linear fashion. Learning songs along the way will gain Naija new powers and even enable her to change form, whereas the items you find scattered around the world can be used to decorate Naija's home.

Mod-support is available, providing tools that let you create your own levels and stories. *Aquaria* won the Seumas McNally Grand Prize at the 2007 Independent Games Festival, and it was also a finalist in three other categories. The game is a commercial download for both PC and Mac.

http://indiegam.es/playAquaria

Zeno Clash

ACE Team

Zeno Clash takes place in the surreal world of Zenozoik, after the hero Ghat has supposedly killed his hermaphroditic parent. Once banished from the city of Halstedom, Gnat sets off with his friend Deadra on a journey of discovery.

Gameplay focuses heavily on first-person melee combat, with players throwing brutal punches and kicks at their opponents. The forests of Zenozoik are filled with a variety of strange creatures known as the Corwid of the Free, and some will attack Gnat on sight. Through flashbacks and revelations, we learn about Gnat's past and why he chose to attack Father-Mother, with many twists and turns in the plot along the way.

In addition to the main story, there's a challenge mode that pits players against hordes of adversaries in a tower, with a final boss on the top floor. *Zeno Clash* is available in versions for PC and the Xbox 360, and a sequel is currently in the works.

http://indiegam.es/playZenoClash

Gish

Cryptic Sea

Gish is out on a stroll with his girlfriend Brea when she is pulled into the subterranean sewers of Dross by a mysterious figure. Of course, Gish jumps straight in to save her—although he's not your usual kind of hero. Gish is, in fact, a ball of tar.

As it turns out, being a ball of tar in a sewage system has its advantages, since Gish has a variety of special abilities that will aid his progress. As enemies attack, he can stick to walls and ceilings or become more fluid and slide through tight gaps in the brickwork. Gish can also contract and expand quickly so that he can leap over gaps, and he can make himself heavy enough to blast through obstacles. Dynamic fluid mechanics give the hero a wonderfully slushy feel.

A versus mode is also included, offering two players the opportunity to do battle and knock each other out of a series of special arenas. Winner in multiple categories at the 2005 Independent Games Festival, *Gish* is a commercial download for PC and Mac.

http://indiegam.es/playGish

Cogs

Lazy 8 Studios

Cogs takes the tried-and-true concept of sliding-tile puzzles and takes it to the next level, with gorgeous steampunk visuals and full three-dimensional rotation around each puzzle. In each puzzle, cogs are attached to tiles that must be lined up in order to complete a series of tasks.

Each level has different objectives, which range from the simple to the insane. Earlier challenges will have you creating chains of cogs, while later on you'll be blasting rockets into space and powering all sorts of crazy contraptions. Puzzles are not confined to a single plane, either—you'll be presented with cubes that have sliding tiles on each face, and even tiles with cogs on the front and back that must be configured simultaneously.

At the first ever Indie Game Challenge Awards *Cogs* took home three cash prizes, including the Professional Grand Prize. The puzzler is available for download in versions for PC, Mac, the iPhone, and the iPad.

http://indiegam.es/playCogs

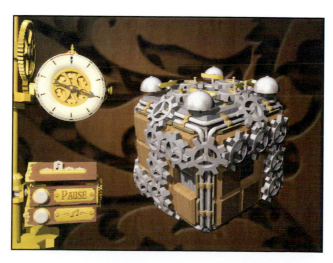

Crayon Physics Deluxe

Petri "Kloonigames" Purho

Imagine if your drawings could come to life. This idea is the basis for *Crayon Physics Deluxe*, in which you attempt to move a ball towards a star by using objects you've drawn in the surrounding environment.

The game is presented as crayon drawings on a folded-out piece of paper, and it allows you to draw any shapes you desire, and even join objects together by using pivots and ropes. Everything you draw is affected by gravity, which can be used to move the ball along. There is no single method for completing any level; you can draw a few simple blocks to nudge the ball to the goal, or illustrate whole scenes and contraptions from cars to catapults to get it rolling. A level editor comes with the game so that you can make your own puzzles and share techniques with friends.

Crayon Physics Deluxe won the Seumas McNally Grand Prize at the Independent Games Festival in 2008 and is available for PC and the iPhone. It was based on an original Experimental Gameplay Project submission called *Crayon Physics*, which is still available for free download.

http://indiegam.es/playCPD

Lugaru HD

Wolfire Games

Turner is an anthropomorphic rabbit with some serious martial-arts training. After his family is brutally murdered by raiders, he embarks on a quest for revenge and discovers a huge conspiracy involving the leaders of the rabbits and evil wolves.

Much of the game is based around hand-to-hand combat, with punches, kicks, disarms, and reversals. Using a combination of button presses and attacks (and the occasional weapon and the stealthy approach), you can fend off multiple enemies at a time. The game features ragdoll physics, allowing for a mixture of lifelike yet exaggerated combat. A challenge mode is included that dispenses with the storyline and puts the player up against a series of increasingly difficult antagonists.

Several hardcore *Lugaru* fans have created mods that provide entirely new stories to play through—in fact, a designer named Tim Soret created HD textures for the entire game, which are now included as standard. The game is available for PC and Mac, and a sequel called *Overgrowth* is currently in the works.

http://indiegam.es/playLugaruHD

Gemini Rue

Joshua Nuernberger

Formerly known as *Boryokudan Rue*, Joshua Nuernberger's futuristic adventure game follows the story of two very different men whose lives become entangled. Azriel Odin is searching for his brother in the Gemini System, while a prisoner known only as Delta-Six tries his hardest to remember his past.

These men hold the key to saving the galaxy from a corruption that's endemic. Players control these characters as they explore more than 60 hand-drawn, film-noir-style scenes in traditional point-and-click adventure gaming fashion. Yet there are plenty of action scenes thrown into the mix as well, with shoot-outs and chases galore that might end with you biting the bullet. It's not often that you get to embark on an adventure with this much charm and variety.

With a plot full of exciting twists and turns, not to mention full voice-acting throughout, *Gemini Rue* heralds a new breed of adventure gaming. The game is available for PC.

http://indiegam.es/playGeminiRue

Everyday Shooter

Jonathan Mak

Although it presents itself simply as an abstract arena blaster, *Everyday Shooter* soon exhibits another facet of its personality through its deep correlation between gameplay and music. You are a little dot in a sea of psychedelic backdrops and adversaries, staying alive by destroying anything that moves.

Each time you kill an enemy, a random note or guitar riff will ring out, thereby creating procedurally-generated music as you play. The riffs harmonise over the soundtrack and create a unique musical experience for every playthrough. Each level features different tracks that you can experiment with; hence the game's description as "an album of games." Players can unlock an assortment of game modes, including a shuffle mode that works like an mp3 player's shuffle feature, and an invincible style of play that's perfect for putting the gameplay aside and enjoying the concept to its fullest.

Everyday Shooter won three awards at the 2007 Independent Games Festival including—not surprisingly—the Excellence In Audio Award. The game is available in versions for PC, the Playstation 3, and Playstation Portable.

http://indiegam.es/playES

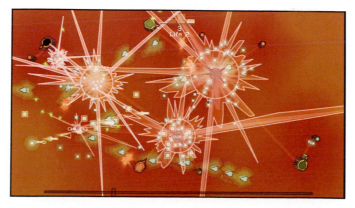

SpaceChem

Zachtronics Industries

SpaceChem is the leading chemical synthesizer company, and you are one of its most hard-working reactor engineers. Your job is to create compounds and substances that can then be shipped to suppliers—and this is just as difficult as it sounds.

Each factory houses a grid that your "waldos" use to travel around so that they can collect atoms, fuse them together, and dump the finished product for future use. Once each factory has been designed, pipelines must be built to ferry the molecules around. *SpaceChem* is a seriously clever and fiendishly tricky puzzler that will really make you sit back and think—it even comes with a periodic table for quick reference! However, it is not necessary to know chemistry to play, and anyone can enjoy the challenging scenarios on offer.

Available for PC and Mac download, *SpaceChem* can initially feel rather overwhelming. Given time, though, it proves itself to be an essential puzzle-gaming experience.

http://indiegam.es/playSpaceChem

Blueberry Garden

Erik Svedäng

Take a stroll through the *Blueberry Garden*, a dream-like world of exploration and curiosities. Some forgetful soul has left a huge tap running, and the rising water now threatens to turn the garden into the next long-lost city of Atlantis.

What at first appears to be a simple platformer soon reveals itself to be unlike anything you've ever played before: a surreal world with its own living, breathing ecosystem. Our beaked hero must use his ability to soar above the ground to help him collect the most random of objects (from giant apples to flash cameras), pile them all up in the centre of the world, and then reach the tap and save the land. The various fruit and berries scattered around the world can also be digested to give the hero special powers and aid his progress.

You'll get one of two different endings, depending on how high your tower reaches. *Blueberry Garden* was the winner of the Seumas McNally Grand Prize at the 2009 Independent Games Festival, and is available for PC-only download.

http://indiegam.es/playBG

Played all 250? Hungry for more indie gaming? Keep up to date on all the latest news, reviews, and indie game releases at IndieGames.com.

Index of Games